Introduction to the

Probation

Service

Dick Whitfield is chief probation officer of Kent. He is the editor of *The State of the Prisons: 200 Years On* (Routledge, 1991) and co-editor with David Scott of *Paying Back: Twenty Years of Community Service* (Waterside Press, 1993). He is also the author of *Tackling the Tag: The Electronic Monitoring of Offenders* (Waterside Press, 1997).

Introduction to the **Probation Service**

Published 1998 by
WATERSIDE PRESS
Domum Road
Winchester SO23 9NN
Telephone or Fax 01962 855567
INTERNET:106025.1020@compuserve.com

ISBN Paperback 1 872 870 73 2

Cataloguing-in-Publication Data A catalogue record for this book can be obtained from the British Library

Printing and binding Antony Rowe Ltd, Chippenham.

Introduction to the

Probation Service

SECOND EDITION

Dick Whitfield

Based on an original work by Anthony Osler

WATERSIDE PRESS
WINCHESTER

Acronyms

ACOP	Association of Chief Officers of Probation
ACPO	Assistant chief probation officer
CPC	Central Probation Council
CPO	Chief probation officer
DCPO	Deputy chief probation officer
DIPS	Diploma in Probation Studies
DipSW	Diploma in Social Work
FCWO	Family court welfare officer
HDC	Home detention curfew
HOC	Home Office circular
ISSP	Intensive support and supervision programme
NACRO	National Association for the Care and Resettlement of Offenders
NAPO	National Association of Probation Officers
NDPB	Non-departmental public bodies
NVQ	National Vocational Qualification
PMA	Probation Managers Association
PO	Probation officer
PSO	Probation service officer
PSR	Pre-sentence report
SPO	Senior probation officer
YOT	Young Offender Team

Introduction to the **Probation Service**

CONTENTS

Acknowledgements

The first edition of *Introduction to the Probation Service* was written by Tony Osler at the beginning of 1995 and I owe a great deal to the clear and comprehensive account which that edition contained. I have, in fact, followed his general outline but the amount of change since that time—legislative, political and operational—has been so huge that it was obvious that a simple revision or up-dating would not be sufficient for this new edition.

Many people have helped during the process of re-writing and it would be impossible to name them all. But I have been particularly grateful to Mark Oldfield, Kent Probation Service's Research Officer, for ideas, arguments and a listening ear, throughout; and to Georgie Empson—as always—for her skill in producing clear and simple text from the weekend's untidy heap of manuscript.

The aim of the book is, simply, to provide an accessible picture of the Probation Service and to give an understanding of what it does, to prospective employees and students, to the interested public, and to sentencers and others with whom we work, day-to-day. It is certainly not a text book, although it will steer you in the direction of more detailed, technical information if you need it.

The figures quoted are as up to date as possible and are taken from:

- *Probation Statistics (England and Wales) 1996* (Home Office, September 1997)
- *Probation Statistics Quarterly Monitor* (Home Office, March 1998)
- *Probation Staffing Statistics: December 1997* (Home Office Research and Statistics Directorate, 1998)
- Reducing Offending: Research Study No. 187 (Home Office, July 1998).

All the reports and extracts from case records are real, but names, dates, locations and identifying details have, of course, been changed. My real debt is to the colleagues and offenders with whom I have worked and from whom I have learned—and who have kept my interest, energy and optimism alive for over 30 years. This book is for them.

Dick Whitfield
July 1998

Introduction

Tuesday was always our main 'Reporting Night'. The probation office was busy for most of the week, with appointments, casual callers, offenders sent by their solicitors or the courts; interviews for pre-sentence reports or for men and women just released from prison; anxious parents or partners—all the usual range of work for a busy probation team in a rapidly expanding New Town. But on Tuesdays, from 3.00 pm until the last person left, usually around 8.30 pm, the office simply heaved. I had, like most of my colleagues, an appointment every 45 minutes or so from 3.00 to 6.00, then a brief rest for tea and gossip, followed by six or more shorter interviews, mostly for offenders nearer the end of their order, who might only be reporting every three or four weeks. For every one who telephoned to apologise or simply missed an appointment (more work in following up the absence later) there was usually an unexpected caller, too—a family crisis, a job lost, a new problem, perhaps—because everyone knew we were there, and available.

The afternoon session was usually the more difficult of the two—the longer interviews were planned for those who were both unemployed and needing the extra time, whereas the evening often ended with the best risks—offenders I had got to know well in the preceding months but who were now in work, confident they could stay out of trouble and content that a brief progress report was all that was needed. It was a turbulent, exhausting day. I had often spent the morning in the magistrates' court—but Tuesdays were the high spot of the week; interviews were often challenging and difficult, but the 'buzz' and satisfaction from helping offenders work on their own problems and believe in their ability to make good was what stayed on the journey home. Small gains—an issue faced or resolved, some evidence of changed attitudes or behaviour, even a job held down or a fine instalment paid for another week—were carefully noted and continuing plans laid. Dogged, patient work mostly, lit with moments of insight or tragedy or humour. And never, ever, dull.

Almost 30 years later, by now chief probation officer in Kent, I stood in for an absent colleague on a reporting night, simply because the local team were stretched almost beyond capacity—and I wanted to see how much had changed. Dealing temporarily with someone else's caseload is never the same—some people will simply not be able to trust a strange face; others may find it refreshing to open up to someone new. Previous records have to be scanned at high speed between interviews to make sure you know what the real issues are. And you have to be interested but sceptical, trusting without being naïve, and patient enough to let offenders go at their own pace if you are to be any use at all.

It was reassuring to find out how much was still familiar. There is much more specialist help available now, from the 'in-house' employment advice team to the local literacy project, which grapples with the vital but painstaking task of helping adults who missed out on basic learning at school to acquire it, much more painfully, in order to survive in a more competitive world. There are specialist agencies to deal with drug and alcohol problems. But there need to be. The level of substance abuse, of long term unemployment, of alienation and poverty and hopelessness are much more widespread, too. It seemed characteristic that my evening ended with an unscheduled visit from a man released from prison just five days earlier—drunk, aggressive, frightened and frustrated in turn. He had failed to find proper accommodation, his 'friends' no longer wanted to know . . . and only prison seemed to beckon. Two cups of coffee . . . a call to the night shelter . . . enough for a sandwich and a lift to his bed for the night. He left, mumbling thanks and clutching an appointment card for the morning, when the real work of trying to help him stay out of trouble would begin.

Some things do not change. The world in which the probation service operates is the real world of social change and conflict, crime and human frailty. Structures, laws, expectations and organizational requirements *do* change at often bewildering speed but *people*— offenders, victims, parents, friends, employers, sentencers—are the threads which are constant and which run through this book. Because change is always with us, and because we can expect it to continue, there was no 'right' time to prepare this text, no pause in which I could define, absolutely, what probation work *is*.

It is, in fact, infinitely adaptable and its survival through a century of change is witness to this. It is, however, not simply subject to some of the transient fashions which appear all too often in policy documents, legislation and public debate. *What* we do in trying to help offenders improve their personal and social situations, in ensuring court orders are observed, and in helping to reduce the risk of reoffending is as constant a thread as the people themselves. *How* we do it has been much more variable and it is right that techniques and methods should change as evidence grows on what works best, and what approaches are needed for new situations.

The need for careful assessment, for good links with sentencers, for good local knowledge of the offender's community and the resources which it contains are as important as ever. So is the overall role for the

Probation Service. The Home Office Research Study 'Reducing Re-offending' (HORS No. 187, 1998) looked at half a century of research on the effectiveness of dealing with offending behaviour. Published at a time when the prison population was at an unsustainably high level, it promised no 'quick fix'—there are no single, simple solutions, but a complex mix of shorter term initiatives and long term programmes which will help to reduce crime. Reconviction rates, overall, are similar for community penalties and the much more expensive use of prison; within those global figures, however, there is growing evidence that some types of intervention can be much more effective in reducing future offending.

The most effective probation programmes, producing up to 15 or 20 per cent lower reconviction rates were identified as those which were skill-based, improved problem solving or drew on behavioural techniques to reinforce improved conduct. These will increasingly become the basis for future probation work, whether centred on individual contact or group programmes. The same report noted, on the community service schemes (CS) run by probation services, that offenders who viewed the CS experience positively were less often reconvicted, and that many felt that they had acquired new skills and a real sense of satisfaction in having helped someone, albeit through a court order.

There is clearly much on which to build and in the conclusion to this book I have tried to suggest what might lie ahead. Current preoccupations with money and with structure, including the wholesale reorganization of the service, are unlikely to be resolved quickly. But they will have much more impact on the framework within which staff operate —rather less on the day-to-day work which is described here.

In her *Handbook of Probation* (1935), which sits on my desk, Mrs Le Mesurier concluded by writing:

> It has been no part of our object here to sing the praises of the probation system with lyrical enthusiasm, but rather to examine it soberly and critically. It is a thing so large in its conception and so immensely potent in its effect on the hopes and happiness of thousands of human lives every year that perhaps it is better not even to try . . . but to be content . . . to let its deeds praise it.

That still seems to me a reasonable hope.

CHAPTER 1

A Brief History

Various ingenious explanations have been put forward to trace the origins of probation right back through the ages to a tenth century statute of Athelstane. The reality—like so much of the probation world—is more confusing and more pragmatic. The United Nations report which described probation's origins as being dependent on 'individual practical experimentation rather than a set of philosophical principles' was probably nearest the truth.

There have been many attempts, over the centuries, to demonstrate that mercy is more effective than severity; that being concerned for the individual has positive effects for the whole community. Even when the law seemed to be at its most savage, exceptions could always be made to reduce the use of capital punishment, mutilation or, later, imprisonment. The landmarks which moved this forward to what we now call probation become more recognisable from about 1820. Then, magistrates in Warwickshire started the practice of releasing suitable young offenders with a purely nominal sentence of one day's imprisonment, providing they returned to their parents or masters. An additional condition, however, was that they should be better supervised in future.

Twenty years later, Matthew Davenport Hill, in Birmingham, released young offenders who appeared before him to the care, and homes, of people willing to act as guardians, provided he thought there was a good prospect of change. He made periodic enquiries as to their progress and, according to official records, only 78 of 483 young people so released, over a period of 17 years, reappeared in court. Still later, the Recorder of Portsmouth, Edward Cox, developed the embryo system by appointing a special 'enquiry officer' to supervise those who had been conditionally released.

Similar developments had also taken place on the other side of the Atlantic, where the modern use of the term 'probation' was accepted from about 1878. It was in the same decade that the defining moment took place in this country, too. In 1876 Frederick Rainer, a printer from Hertfordshire, was so appalled by the cycle of 'offence after offence and sentence after sentence' which he saw in the courts that he gave a five shilling donation to the Church of England Temperance Society so that 'something might be done'.

11

The choice of a temperance society was an obvious response to the pattern of heavy drinking, despair and poverty which seemed inextricably linked to petty offending. The Victorian age was a time of rising concern at the level of moral degeneration of the new working class, and that Society's response—to appoint a 'police court missionary' to reclaim drunkards—fitted easily with this. The missionary would interview offenders in the cells, decide who might respond to help and then propose a plan to the court to put this into effect. This revolved around signing a pledge to give up alcohol, finding proper accommodation and employment and accepting supervision by the missionary over a set period of time.

It also worked. Courts came to rely on the dedicated individuals who used their religious convictions and humanitarian strengths to such good purpose and, by 1900, over one hundred missionaries were operating in urban courts. They were also dealing with far more than drunkards. Mental health problems, chronic unemployment and family conflicts all loom large in early records. But at this stage the approach still relied on voluntary experimentation and use; it was not until 1907 that the Probation of Offenders Act put this work onto a statutory footing.

The early legislation
The path towards legislation had not, in fact, been easy. The Howard Association, forerunner of the modern Howard League, had long been pressing for statutory supervision along the lines already established in Massachusetts, USA for two decades. There, the policy of 'reform without punishment' provided for a probation officer to undertake tasks which would nowadays be immediately recognisable—reports to courts before sentence; supervision, including home visits, periodic progress reports and the power to arrest probationers and return them to court if they broke the conditions of their probation.

In this country, however, a first attempt to follow suit—the Probation of First Offenders Act 1887—contained no element of actual supervision. It also attracted hostility in Parliament, including the objection to allowing '. . . a lot of amateurs to say that persons who have been convicted should be allowed quietly to merge into the honest, peaceful population'.

By 1907, however, the missionaries—quietly and effectively—had made their point. The new Act made probation available to all criminal courts and for all offences except murder and treason. It required the consent of the offender. In addition to standard conditions:

12

- to keep in touch as directed
- to lead an honest and industrious life
- to be of good behaviour and keep the peace

an order could include a wide range of other conditions, from the Draconian to the unenforceable. (The latter, such as a condition 'not to associate with undesirable persons or frequent undesirable places' might be dismissed as a quaint, old fashioned idea. But it re-surfaced in 1989 legislation in Queensland which specifically prohibits 'community release' offenders from attendance at 'racing or gaming establishments, turf clubs, dog tracks, casinos, massage parlours or similar establishments . . .').

The scope of the 1907 Act could hardly have been wider and the vision of those who drafted it was matched by the use to which it was put. It was this same act which laid down the basic duty of the probation officer—to 'advise, assist and befriend' those being supervised. This was something much more practical than a vague impulse towards philanthropy; the words may have changed and the framework altered but the ideals of the 1907 Act in terms of individual help and rehabilitation are surprisingly intact. Whether they will continue to survive in the face of current political pressures is an issue to which we will return.

A period of growth

The 1907 Act also gave powers to courts to appoint and pay probation officers, although it was some time before the original police court missionaries were either absorbed into the new service or replaced. Not all courts saw the need, either, and it was not until 1925 that it became a *requirement* that the services of one or more probation officers should be available for every court.

By then, a period of steady growth was already apparent. 8000 probation orders were made in 1908; 15,094 in 1925 and nearly 19,000 in 1933. By the early 1920's about half the national caseload comprised juveniles under 16, but probation officers were involved in a much wider range of work—the supervision of children in need of care and protection, social inquiry reports, matrimonial conciliation and the supervision of offenders released from some prison sentences; even fine supervision orders, to try and avoid the sanction of imprisonment for non-payment.

It was a period, too, which saw a move away from the religious, missionary ideal towards a more professionally based service. There was still a belief in the advice, assistance and befriending at the heart of the work—but a recognition that proper diagnosis, assessment and treatment should inform all that was done. Above all, it was a period of very uneven growth. Some courts had appointed only part-time officers; many of the full-time staff in post were unqualified, inexperienced or overworked (or all three). Far too many areas had no woman probation officer available and the administrative and support arrangements were often inadequate. It was not until 1936, with the Departmental Committee on the Social Services in Courts of Summary Jurisdiction, that a more coherent framework emerged.

The Committee recommended that probation should remain a locally controlled service, but that the Home Office should play a greater part in its organization and direction. A probation inspectorate was established, more emphasis was placed on reports to courts and a Probation Training Board and Central Advisory Committee were formed. Supervisory arrangements were made (subject to Home Office approval), leading to the appointment of senior and principal probation officers. The foundations of a full time, professional service had been laid.

The Criminal Justice Act 1948

The 1948 Act was a watershed. It incorporated all the hopes and principles of the emerging Welfare State. It repealed all past legislation in respect of probation and set about defining properly the issues surrounding procedure, organization, finance and practice. It recognised that the struggles of the inter-war years to get probation known, accepted, understood and used by the courts were largely over—and it set the service firmly in the social climate of the time. Training opportunities were improved, links with courts were strengthened, new probation committees organized and approved probation hostels and homes brought within the scope of public funds. Probation had now come of age; the eminent criminologist, Radzinowicz, wrote, just ten years later:

> If I were asked: 'What is the most significant contribution made by this country to the new penological theory and practice which struck root in the twentieth century?' . . . my answer would be probation. (Preface to *The Results of Probation*, MacMillan, 1958)

The onus was now firmly on the scientific assessment and treatment of the individual, in one-to-one casework. The probation officer had come to be seen as a professional caseworker, using skills developed in common with other social workers, but applied in a specialised field.

Thereafter, development and growth were more or less continuous. Duties proliferated, training arrangements were again strengthened;

and, perhaps most significantly the higher courts (then Assizes and Quarter Sessions—now the Crown Court) were each allocated a probation officer so that its use could develop with more serious offenders.

Milestones
We have become used to major criminal justice legislation almost every year, at present. Whether the sheer quantity is matched by the quality is rather more arguable. For three decades following the 1948 Act, however, time was usually allowed between major legislative change (sometimes up to five years) and there are thus a series of recognisable milestones which point to the development of the modern probation service throughout this period. The main ones were:

- **1961** *The Streatfeild Report* which recommended a greater use of social enquiry reports (forerunner to pre-sentence reports, or PSRs) in all courts
- **1962** *The Morison Report* which led to more research on the work of the service.
- **1966** *Work in prisons* became an integral part of the probation service's task (*Chapter 7*).
- **1968** *Parole was introduced.* Probation officers supervised parolees on release from prison and also wrote reports as part of the selection process.
- **1973** *Community service* by offenders was introduced (*Chapter 5*).

By the end of the 1970s, however, storm clouds were on the horizon. In 1974 an American criminologist Robert Martinson published an article 'What Works? Questions and Answers About Prison Reform'. This produced a very pessimistic assessment of the effectiveness of a whole range of treatment provision, which was generally taken to conclude that, in fact, *nothing* works; or not very much at all. The following years saw a collective loss of confidence in what the probation service could hope to achieve and this seemed to be confirmed by disappointing results from a whole range of studies including the Home Office 'Impact' study in this country and those of a number of similarly intensive programmes of supervision in the USA.

It was, however, a sweeping conclusion and not sustained when the evidence was reassessed in detail, as Martinson later admitted. Rather more positive evidence was produced about *some* approaches which work for *some* people. But the damage had been done. The overall picture was not helped by a lack of rigorous and detailed research into probation programmes and—given the time lapse before reconviction data can be assembled—it was some time before alternative, authoritative views could be heard.

There is, now, a significant body of evidence about how more effective supervision of offenders in the community can be organized. Some programmes *do* work, and the best of these may reduce reoffending by around 25 per cent. To do so, they need to be:

- clearly targeted on offending behaviour
- consistently delivered by well trained staff
- relevant to offenders' problems and needs
- equally relevant to the participants' learning styles.

Even then, there are many factors which may affect success or failure, and a much more comprehensive approach to planning and delivering and evaluating the outcomes—known under the generic term of 'What Works?', or 'Strategies for Effective Offender Supervision' is now in place. In the meantime, the political and social landscape was changing, too, as some of the later milestones show:

- **1984** *First Statement of National Objectives and Priorities*
  This was the first attempt to produce a coherent framework of provision from over 50 separate, independent and autonomous probation areas. It was long overdue. It now seems incredibly tentative, both in scope and in the way it was introduced (the home secretary 'hoped' committees and chief probation officers would 'take full account of these objectives and priorities, as seen from here' as they developed their area plans). But the statement seemed radical at the time and presaged an era of slowly growing central controls and—ultimately—a politicisation of the direction which the probation service would be required to take.

- **1988** *Green Paper: Punishment, Custody and the Community*
  This, followed by the White Paper, *Crime, Justice and Protecting the Public* (1990) took enormous strides in questioning the need for the extensive use of custody on which this country seemed to be set. It sought to promote a greater use of community-based options, particularly for burglary and theft; equally it promoted a comprehensive shift in the way young adult offenders might be dealt with. John Patten, the then Home Office minister, argued that we had to move to a new way of dealing with non-violent, less serious offenders and asked: 'Can the Probation Service move centre stage in the criminal justice system?'

- **1989** *Audit Commission Report: The Probation Service—Promoting Value for Money*
  This report provided an answer to John Patten's question. It was 'Yes'. This was not an unequivocal endorsement but it was very positive about the skills and methods which had been developed and added '. . . examples abound of creative and imaginative initiatives' for dealing with offenders. But it was critical of the limited amount of evaluation of programmes which took place; the *ad hoc* way in which good practice developed but was not spread; and the generally confused and unaccountable structure which was in place. The report produced a 'framework for probation intervention' which has since had wide acceptance.

Identify offender characteristics	Recommend appropriate intervention	Work with offender	Monitor offending pattern
Assessment	**Court**	**Supervision**	**Evaluate outcomes**

- **1991** *Criminal Justice Act*
  The 1991 Act, a bold and forward thinking piece of legislation, set out to do much more than ensure probation's place 'centre-stage'. It recognised prison as negative and expensive and sought to develop—through 'punishment in the community'—a new philosophy whereby offenders would receive their 'just deserts', or punishment proportionate to the seriousness of the offence.

  The legislation was given little time to prove itself and was swiftly amended in 1993 and 1994. By this time, sentencing policy itself was centre stage and an unprecedented amount of media and public attention was focused on the issue. 'Tough on crime' became a mantra for both political parties with Michael Howard, the then Conservative home secretary, emphasising that 'prison works', despite the fact that a predecessor had suggested that prison should be regarded as 'an expensive way of making a bad person worse'.

- **1992** *National Standards for the Probation Service*
  The first, clear, national statement of expected practice in both the objectives and process of supervision (revised in 1995). See later chapters for the effect of National Standards on the various community sentences.

17

Current developments
The last few years have seen an unprecedented level of activity and scrutiny, set against growing funding difficulties. The economic problems were not unexpected—the funding of all public services has become more and more difficult and, in fact, cash limited budgets came late to probation. They arrived, however, at a time when expectations of the service, exemplified by National Standards, were rising, and workloads were growing, too. Some of the results of this are discussed in *Chapter 2*. What has, equally, shaped recent history has been the enormous media and political attention which has focused on the work of the service, some of it very hostile indeed.

After a long period during which crime was not seen as a party political issue, it gradually became one of the most contentious. Prison disturbances, miscarriages of justice, 'zero tolerance' policing and other issues all fed the public debate at different times, but it was public concern about levels of crime (whether the fear was real or not, it was certainly perceived) that became a constant thread. Politicians outbid each other in terms of promises to be tough on crime and offenders and there was no shortage of individual cases on which to generalise.

It was a climate in which probation was all too often dismissed as a 'soft option'; a 'let-off' in a system in which only imprisonment offered real punishment, despite the acknowledged demands which probation programmes and community service orders also make. It *is* a climate which has yet to be fully resolved; subsequent chapters look at the current situation and the book finishes with an assessment of the proposals for change and reform that are now under way. Probation has been a very adaptable vehicle in its 100 or so years of operation and this brief history demonstrates how much it has needed to adapt to social changes, new ideas, new work and new opportunities. The difficulties which might arise if change were to be linked to a very different philosophy or sense of values are still a real concern.

A time of change and opportunity
The next chapter describes the service as it was in 1998, and as it will be when staff join under the new training arrangements. The structural and organizational changes which are on the horizon will take some time to be realised, not least because of the need for legislation, and there are realistic fears about the 'planning blight' which a long-drawn out process of change will impose. Those same changes, however, will also bring new opportunities for a wide range of staff and—if well managed—a new strength on which the service can build over the next decade.

18

CHAPTER 2

The Probation Service Today

Probation is an essentially local service. It is organized in 54 different areas, corresponding largely to pre-1998 local government boundaries and with each responding to the particular needs of the area it serves. Each service is governed by a probation committee, answerable to the Home Office; Northern Ireland has a Probation Board and Jersey, Guernsey and the Isle of Man have their own probation services. (In Scotland, the work undertaken by the probation service is done by local authority social services departments). Probation services employ just over 14,000 staff and numbers vary enormously locally, from less than 100 in the smallest services to over 1,000 in Inner London. There is a general recognition that the current fragmentation, and disparities in size, may not be helpful. Discussions on the amalgamation of areas have taken place over the last few years, with Oxfordshire and Buckinghamshire becoming a single service; other areas have chosen more collaborative models, with shared services. The process is clearly not complete. A list of current areas, with their Headquarters addresses, is contained in *Appendix II*.

PURPOSE, VALUES AND RESPONSIBILITIES

Each area service produces its own published plan of local priorities and objectives, but it does so within the framework of a national plan issued by the Home Office which, as the major funder, specifies the home secretary's expectations. The national statement of purposes defines the service's role in the following terms:

The service serves the courts and public by:

- providing reports to the courts
- supervising offenders in the community
- managing offender programmes to ensure offenders lead law abiding lives, in a way that minimises risk to the public
- safeguarding the welfare of children in family proceedings
- helping communities prevent crime and reducing its effects on victims.

Complementing this statement of purpose is a statement on values.

The service is committed to:

- treating all people fairly, openly and with respect
- challenging attitudes and behaviour which result in crime and cause distress to victims
- work for and with communities to reduce crime
- promote the welfare of the family.

There is a real danger that these two short summaries, which have already been subject to some recent amendment, will be devalued by repetition or be lost in the welter of change mentioned in *Chapter 1*. Yet they remain crucial if the service is to remain vital and healthy and able to retain the confidence and respect of everyone—from offenders to sentencers—with whom it deals. For a complex service, it is a short list. Yet it captures both the spirit which inspired the original police court missionaries and the dogged, patient mixture of realism and optimism which underpins the day to day work of the service now. For anyone contemplating work in the service and asking the fundamental questions: 'Is this what I want to do?' and 'Is this how I want to go about it?' these two short summaries of purpose and values should provide clear answers.

The Home Office list of responsibilities is a general one and much of this book is devoted to exploring what the contents of that list mean in practice. It describes the main responsibilities as being to:

- provide the courts with accurate and timely information to assist in all sentencing decisions
- design and supervise community sentences for offenders
- provide places in approved probation/bail hostels
- provide risk assessment and other reports for the Parole Board and the prison service
- prepare prisoners for release from custody and supervise them following their release
- provide welfare reports and mediation as requested by the courts in children's proceedings.

(Source: 'Three Year plan for the Probation Service 1997-2000', Home Office)

THE MAIN TASKS

Translating the list of responsibilities into practice is probably best done by following the criminal justice process through, chronologically, and summarising the part which probation plays.

Crime prevention

Before a crime has even been committed, probation staff are involved in crime prevention activities, with schemes as diverse as crime audits, summer playschemes, community action programmes or targeted work in high crime areas. Probation involvement is small scale in comparison to those with primary responsibility, such as police, social services departments or local authorities, but the value of inter-agency work is increasingly being recognised. New provisions concerning Community Safety Plans, contained in the Crime and Disorder Act 1998, recognise this and probation areas will increasingly be involved in practical measures to prevent or reduce crime.

Decision whether or not to prosecute, or to allow bail

Once an offence has been committed a number of issues need to be considered. If a caution is to be administered, rather than a decision to prosecute through the courts, then especially for younger offenders, probation staff may be involved in assessing the best option.

The question of whether to remand on bail or in custody, pending a full court hearing, is also of fundamental importance. Bail information schemes, run by the service, provide information to prosecutors and to courts to help with this decision. Does the defendant have a proper address? Are there problems with drink or drugs? What are the risks of absconding or of further offending? Answers to these questions will inform the courts so that they can decide whether to grant bail and if so under what, if any, extra conditions. For some offenders this will mean living at a hostel run by the local probation service. There are 101 of these, providing 2,200 beds for people awaiting trial, or for people on a community order, or following release from prison. They provide a supervised environment, with curfews, rules about drinking and drugs and specialist help and advice for the range of difficulties with which offenders usually come. Hostels are dealt with in further detail in *Chapter 5*.

Sentencing

Once an offender has been convicted, the magistrates or judge responsible for the case has the job of deciding the most appropriate sentence. In all cases where prison is a possibility, or the court decides that it would be helpful, a pre-sentence report (PSR) is provided by a probation officer. Possible sentences range from discharges and fines, to probation and community service orders and prison and the task is to advise on suitability and risk through interview, home visits and a range of other information. Over 220,000 PSRs are prepared each year.

Court work is considered in further detail in *Chapter 3*.

21

Community orders
Probation and community service, either on their own or together in the shape of a combination order for more serious offenders, form the core work of the service.

Community service
Community service—an idea pioneered in this country and an approach now to be found in many parts of the world—simply involves offenders of all ages, through unpaid work, in paying back to their local communities for the damage involved in their offence. Punishment thus serves a useful purpose and offenders can find themselves carrying out environmental work, improving local facilities such as community halls or play areas, working with and for the elderly or disabled or a wide range of necessary and imaginative projects. The orders are carried out to National Standards to ensure they are sufficiently rigorous and although about 20 per cent are breached (returned to court) because of new offences or because the conditions have not been kept the benefit to the community (and, often, to offenders themselves) is enormous. In 1997 about 52,000 such orders were imposed; an estimated 17,000 individuals or groups were helped from six million hours of unpaid labour. The orders can be for any period between 40-240 hours.

Communiy service is dealt with in further detail in *Chapter 6*.

Probation
Probation orders can be used for a wide variety of adult offenders and may contain an equally wide range of provision—from individual to group supervision; from personal to family based work; from help with drugs and alcohol to employment, managing money or improving basic education. This can involve complex treatment programmes using other experts like mental health professionals or psychologists or it may be based wholly on a supervision plan drawn up between probation officer and offender, and agreed by the court. All involve an element of confronting the behaviour which resulted in the offence and a plan for avoiding reoffending.

Again, National Standards provide the overall framework on how orders are structured and run, and failure to keep to the conditions means going back to court. In 1997 around 50,000 people (including 10,000 women) were supervised in this way.

Probation is dealt with in further detail in *Chapter 4*.

Other types of community order
Other community orders include supervision orders for younger (10-17 year old) offenders, although this work is largely undertaken by social

services departments. A number of areas of the country have multi-agency teams to deal with the whole range of youth court work and the experience gained has become the blueprint for the future. Youth Offending Teams (known as 'YOTS') using the resources of social services, police, probation, education, youth and community and health services are being set up as the Crime and Disorder Act 1998 becomes law (with piloting of YOTS taking place in selected areas). Probation officers will play a significant part in the new arrangements: see, generally, *Chapter 9.*

Prison work: Before and after release
Over 500 probation service staff are located within prisons. They work with prison staff in sentence planning, making plans for resettlement after release, liaising with probation staff in the offender's home area and running a range of programmes within the prison which, as with community based orders, try to address the underlying cause of offending. For most prisoners, too, probation staff will make assessments about release—whether on parole or licence or subject to electronic tagging under a new Home Detention Curfew scheme—and help devise the conditions necessary to protect the public.

This work has grown remorselessly in recent years, as the prison population itself has risen, and over 66,000 prisoners were released on licence under supervision at some stage in 1997. Prisoners sentenced to more than 12 months custody are supervised on release (known as 'automatic conditional release') and the more serious offenders who are given sentences of four years or more are released under more stringent conditions subject to assessment by the Parole Board ('discretionary conditional release'). For the most serious offenders—those given life sentences—contact with the probation service may have to continue indefinitely and some sex offenders may be given extended periods of post-release licence, too.

Work in prisons and after an offender is released is dealt with in further detail in *Chapters 7* and *8* respectively.

Victims
In recent years, probation services have also been given specific responsibilities in relation to victims of crime. In serious cases involving violence or sentences of four years or more, services contact the victims shortly after the offender is sentenced. This is to provide information and to offer continuing contact during the sentence, and especially as release on licence is considered. Victims' views can be passed on to the appropriate body, such as the Parole Board, especially if there are fears about the offender returning to the same circumstances or

neighbourhood. The work requires real sensitivity but can give victims both the recognition and reassurance they often need. It builds on the long association with Victim Support and represents the probation service's commitment to the *Victims Charter*.

FAMILY WORK

As officers of the court, probation officers also staff the system of family courts in their capacity as family court welfare officers—a sphere of work which currently accounts for about eight per cent of the service's resources. As families go through the painful process of separation and divorce, probation staff try to help courts and parents to ensure that the best possible arrangements are put in place for the children. This is usually done by interview with the children and adults concerned (including grandparents, teachers and doctors) which are distilled and analysed in reports about residence or contact. In some instances, family court welfare officers will see whether problems can be resolved through mediation; they will also try and help children with separated parents by providing contact centres—neutral, safe environments—where meetings and visits can take place.

The scale of this work is considerable—in 1996 over 36,000 reports were prepared for family courts at all levels and dispute resolution was attempted with 53,000 couples. But the debate about whether the work is properly located within an agency, the probation service, whose business is primarily concerned with criminal, rather than civil, justice processes continues. The arguments are by no means one sided but early in 1998 the government announced an inter-departmental review about the future provision of the Family Court Welfare Service which seemed to indicate that the probation service might be replaced by a new agency, perhaps located within the Lord Chancellor's Department.

Work and responsibilities in relation to the family courts are dealt with in further detail in *Chapter 10*.

SETTING OBJECTIVES

The list of tasks is formidable and, in carrying them out and seeking to improve services generally, both individual probation areas and the Home Office have annual objectives and priorities relating to specific issues. For 1998-99 the Home Office published priorities (which may remain for several years) and these are related to three main goals:

Goal A	• reducing crime and supervising offenders effectively
Goal B	• providing high quality information, assessment related services to the courts and other users of the service
Goal C	• fairness and high standards of service delivery
Each of the three goals has set priorities:	
Goal A	• to ensure that community sentences and supervision after release from custody combine effective punishment with success in reducing reoffending • to reduce the risk to the public from dangerous offenders • to improve offenders' access to the job market
Goal B	• to continue to improve the quality of pre-sentence reports in line with National Standards
Goal C	• to continue to improve the management of staff and the use of information and information technology.

NATIONAL AND LOCAL ARRANGEMENTS

The current structure of national policy but local accountability; nationally determined funding but local operational management; and National Standards of supervision but local discretion clearly has some scope for tension. It exists, and successive moves towards a more centralised service have heightened the tension while local areas remain the building blocks on which the service is built. These are unlikely to be resolved until wider decisions on the future structure of the service are made. In the meantime, widely trailed suggestions have included 're-branding' the service as the National Corrections Agency (thus emphasising the punishment and control functions), re-naming orders to improve public understanding and to enhance their credibility, opening all levels of the service to a wider range of applicants and much closer working relationships with a range of other bodies, but particularly the prison service.

There are some serious issues about working towards a more coherent criminal justice *system*, rather than a collection of independent agencies, and about achieving more consistency nationally. There is also a good deal of 'sound bite' material related to the perceptions of politicians, rather than the public. It may be to everyone's advantage to

25

rename the probation order a 'community supervision order' and the community service order a 'sentenced work order'; at least the new names describe accurately their respective aims. Whether or not a more fundamental change, from an overall name known for 90 years, would have any real impact on public perception is much more arguable.

In the meantime, the balance between national and local 'players' rests between the bodies who are briefly described now.

The Home Office
The Probation Unit of the Home Office describes its function as to

> develop and promote government policy on the supervision of offenders in the community and other aspects of probation service work; and to assist individual probation services to serve the courts and the public in an efficient and effective way.

In practice, the role and influence of the Home Office have increased substantially through cash limits, training and appraisal arrangements, the development of National Standards, requirements in terms of activity recording and statistical returns, the collection of data on serious incidents, the development of a national information technology strategy . . . and in many other ways. This is hardly surprising—he who pays the piper tends also to allocate and determine resources in accordance with pre-determined policy objectives. But much of the work of the service does not stem from central government. It comes from magistrates and judges, all properly independent, who must be satisfied that work in local areas retains the confidence of courts and communities alike. And the neat and orderly world of civil servants is far removed from the messy, complex and unpredictable business of dealing with difficult and disturbed offenders.

Yet there *is* a balance worth working for. Few measures are arbitrarily dumped on an unwilling service and the process of consultation between the Home Office and probation organizations, whilst not always smooth, is constant and achieves a large measure of understanding.

The Probation Inspectorate
This is an independent inspectorate within the Home Office, which reports to the home secretary and publishes its reports. In addition to actual inspections it promotes high standards of management and practice and advises the Home Office on a range of probation matters. Most inspectors (though not all) are drawn from within the ranks of area probation services and this wide-ranging experience is important

in the detailed work they undertake. They look at the outputs and performance of individual services, assessing quality and value for money; they also seek to establish whether the services received by courts, prisons, offenders and the public are meeting needs and being delivered in the most effective way possible. Generally there are two kinds of inspections:

- *Quality and effectiveness (Q and E) inspections* which concentrate on a particular area service (each area should have such an inspection about once every five years). Not all aspects of work can be covered but, in addition to a general assessment of the service, some aspects of work or specialist tasks will be examined in depth. Detailed recommendations are made to the chief probation officer and the probation committee. A follow-up inspection takes place 18 months later to ensure that action has been taken.

- *Thematic Inspections,* when a particular area of work, nationally, is examined through a sample of 10 or 12 probation areas. Recent 'thematics' have covered: work with sex offenders; difficult and dangerous offenders; community service; and court work. Recommendations follow to all services, on the basis of what has been found.

The work of the service is also open to other kinds of scrutiny—the Audit Commission being, probably, the most perceptive and important in an era where value for money in public services is, rightly, a continuing preoccupation.

Area Probation Committees
Each probation area employs its own staff and is supervised by a probation committee. This mainly comprises representatives of the magistrates for the area, together with at least one member of the judiciary, generally a circuit judge. The local authorities, who contribute financially to the service, are also represented and co-opted members, who may represent a wide range of special interests and expertise, are allocated a percentage of places in relation to the size of the overall committee. There is, therefore, the possibility of a very wide range of local citizens on the committee, for magistrates may also be, e.g. housewives, teachers, farmers, trade union officials, business people or doctors—as, indeed, my own committee members have been. Local authority representatives may also be able to offer particularly effective links, perhaps with the social services committee; and co-opted members can offer the skills which are needed in even the best

27

organized committee—in Kent they have at various times included a lecturer from a local University social work course, the Prison Service area manager, the chair of the county Victim Support scheme, a defence solicitor and an employment law specialist.

The committee holds the chief probation officer to account for the work of the service and approves policy. It receives regular reports and, in many areas, sees a good deal of the work of the service at first hand. It can represent the service in many ways, not least because its magistrate members are also active in local benches. At their best, Committees are well informed, concerned, supportive (but not uncritical) and a crucial link between the service and the community it serves.

Yet committees have attracted considerable criticism—for being unrepresentative of the whole community, for being too large and unwieldy, for not holding chief officers to account sufficiently, and being insufficiently involved in strategic planning. In 1993 the then home secretary announced that they would be replaced by smaller 'probation boards', with approved members, paid chairs and with the chief probation officer as a full member. Having encouraged area services to move towards this model (which a number did with some enthusiasm) the Home Office spent the next few years regretting that it had been 'unable to find Parliamentary time' to bring in legislation to implement the changes. (This despite managing to produce Criminal Justice Bills, usually with more than 100 clauses, on an annual basis). The 'shadow boards' are thus in limbo—often working effectively, but with formal power still constituted in the committee. The situation seems unlikely to be resolved before full scale, structural change is imposed on the service.

Liaison committees
At local level, individual benches or groups of benches use liaison committees to keep channels of communication with sentencers (i.e. judges and magistrates) open, to share joint concerns, to undertake joint training and generally to keep well informed. They were originally known as 'case committees', a title which accurately described their function—they met quarterly and, originally, simply reviewed every case with the supervising officer concerned. Decisions about breach or early discharge for good progress were made in this setting and simply confirmed in court later. This was eventually decided to be inappropriate (as well as impracticable, as caseloads and numbers of officers grew) and more general functions, as described above, replaced the old agenda.

28

The result has not been wholly positive and liaison committees vary considerably in terms of commitment, attendance and sense of purpose. At best, they cement relationships locally, lead to a shared understanding of the very different roles that magistrates and probation officers have to play, and develop mutual trust. They are certainly worth a real investment of time and effort, particularly in large urban benches where the chance of a particular magistrate meeting a particular probation officer more than once a year (let alone each understanding the other better) is remote.

STAFFING STRUCTURES

Like every other aspect of the service, staff structures are changing. The service traditionally had a relatively flat, broad structure with most members of staff having direct contact with offenders. The majority of staff were main grade officers, working in the community in teams managed by a senior probation officer (often called an SPO) and while that basic structure remains, a number of factors have been responsible for change.

First there has been a tendency towards greater specialisation. This has always been an option—court work, specialist report writers, family court teams, sex offender specialists, group workers and staff concentrating on prison throughcare work have often been the basis for very effective service provision. Then, in 1995 Michael Howard, the home secretary, announced that the qualifying training scheme for probation officers, the Diploma in Social Work (Dip SW), was to be abandoned. His aim was to reduce the social work base of the service and open up probation work to a much wider range of people—recently retired or redundant NCOs from the armed forces were usually mentioned—in line with government plans to 'toughen up' community sentences. A difficult period followed, in which the supply of newly qualified probation officers dried up, and negotiations on a new qualification stalled. These are only now (Spring 1998) being resolved. A full description of the new arrangements can be found in *Appendix I* to this work. The impact of this period of planning blight would have been much worse had it not taken place at a time when, because of cuts in the cash limits, area probation services were also having to reduce staff numbers.

The following table gives some idea of the way financial difficulties have had to be reflected in staffing cuts.

England and Wales	1994	1995	1996	1997
Probation officers	7800	7312	7455	7171
Other probation staff	8700	7922	8246	7660

Probation Officers and Other Probation Staff in Post Each Year (December)

Within these depressing figures (because, at the same time, workloads were rising) other trends were also apparent. Administrative staff represented nine per cent of all non-probation officer posts in December 1997, having grown by two per cent in five years. Clerical and secretarial staff represented 42 per cent, having fallen by five per cent over the same period.

In 1989 female probation officers made up 42 per cent of the total; ten years later the figure was 53 per cent. In the same period, among probation officers above main grade the proportion has risen even faster, from 23 per cent to 39 per cent.

The service is built on two main groups of staff—probation officers and probation service officer/probation assistant (PSO) grade staff. This latter, very confusing title, covers a wide variety of posts and task undertaken by staff who are not qualified as probation officers but may nevertheless have real expertise in specific fields. They include:

- community service officers, and the sessional supervisors who run community service groups
- PSO staff providing general support to field work and court teams, specialist probation court representatives, victim liaison staff, drug and alcohol specialists; bail information and accommodation workers and a range of other posts for which a social work qualification may not be needed
- hostel assistant wardens and support staff.

Probation officers normally start their careers by undertaking the full range of field work and, indeed, the first year is characterised by a reduced caseload and carefully supervised practice before confirmation in post is achieved after 12 months. That confirmation may be delayed or refused if a sufficient standard of work is not reached but there should be no surprises at the 12 month mark for regular supervision by a senior probation officer should have identified strengths and weaknesses well before the final inspection leading to confirmation.

30

Once some experience has been gained, moves to specialist posts are usually available. As already indicated, work in courts, prisons and in family court teams are covered in later chapters, but there are also a wide range of other tasks which may lead to wholly or partly specialist work—group work, specialist work with drug and alcohol problems or with sex offenders are probably the most common examples.

Senior probation officer
The majority of staff work in the community in teams led by a senior probation officer (SPO). Whether the team covers the full range of field work or has a specialist function, the SPO will have some common tasks as the local manager:

- the organization of the team and its workload, with the necessary administrative support
- supervision of individual staff. All probation areas have regular evaluation and appraisal procedures; there are also mechanisms for regular review, with the probation officer concerned, of the most dangerous and high risk offenders
- acting as the link with courts and other criminal justice agencies locally, and with voluntary bodies and others who have an interest in offenders and crime prevention
- interpreting area policy to staff, keeping them advised of legislative and other changes and making sure that senior staff, too, are aware of the impact of these changes.

It is, like many middle management posts, a key position—close enough for some involvement in day to day practice but also able to share in the development of policy at area level.

Higher grade officers
Assistant chief probation officers (ACPOs) are responsible for groups of SPOs and may well have specialist responsibility for developing specific areas of work, such as training or internal inspections and quality control. The largest areas may well also have one or more deputy chief probation officers (DCPOs) to ensure that operational management can be properly achieved. And each service, of course, needs to draw on financial, personnel, administrative and property expertise, research and information staff, public relations skills and the host of 'support' activities which are actually central to a well managed organization. The total cost of the Probation Service in England and Wales was over £400 million in 1997/8 and of course budgets vary enormously depending on the size of the area covered. The largest,

Inner London, has an annual budget of over £40 million; a large urban area like West Yorkshire around £16 million; a large shire county over £10 million and smaller services, like Cornwall or Shropshire have budgets of under £3 million.

Leading each service is a chief probation officer (CPO) who is accountable, through the local probation committee for the work of the service in his or her own area. This includes the allocation of resources, ensuring that the service operates within its cash limit, the development and maintenance of high standards of work, good information systems, public relations and the publication of an annual report so that the service can properly account for its use of public money, and the work it does, to both the home secretary and the local community.

Until 1994, every CPO came from a probation service background and progressed through the ranks of senior and assistant chief probation officer over a number of years. The government then signalled that it would allow committees to appoint suitable managers from industry, commerce and other disciplines and the first such appointment (to an ex-submarine Commander) was made at the end of that year. It remains the only external appointment (as at the time of writing). The fact that the option is now available, however, reinforces the point which this brief sketch of current activity should reinforce— that the modern probation service is a complex, staff-intensive operation that needs to keep two strands in balance. First, that in dealing with difficult and dangerous offenders, in using significant sums of public money and in discharging some very specific accountabilities to both the courts and the local community it needs to be well managed if it is to merit the confidence placed in it. Second, that in dealing with a wide range of people who may also be troubled, chaotic, vulnerable or confused, and over whom it has considerable powers, it must discharge those responsibilities to the very highest standards.

Social work values are not empty promises or a symptom of being soft on crime; treating people fairly, openly and with respect and recognising their capacity for growth and change are also an essential part of a civilised society. 'Getting tough on crime' has been an all party slogan for too long, for unless it asks 'What works?', 'What can be effective in reducing offending?', 'What is needed to overcome disadvantage and to make excluded young people, in particular, see the benefits of working to become law abiding citizens?', then all we are doing is storing up worse problems for tomorrow. The probation service is only part of the complex jigsaw of criminal justice, but it does have a crucial part to play. Andrew Rutherford made the point with brutal clarity in his book *Criminal Justice and the Pursuit of Decency*

(Waterside Press, 1993). Humane values have to lie at the heart of the system, he wrote, adding:

> the expression of humane values within criminal justice ultimately resides with practitioners. Indeed in the absence of such values, criminal justice invariably descends into apathy and, ultimately, violence.

That is why, despite its quaint sounding phraseology 'advise, assist and befriend', the phrase from the Probation of Offenders Act 1907 (see *Chapter 1*) is just as relevant today. It includes holding people accountable for their actions, enforcing the conditions of an order and being both tough and realistic in the face of individual difficulties and public risk. But rehabilitation pays dividends in both human and financial terms and today's probation services have to demonstrate that these values and principles can be translated into practice.

CHAPTER 3

In and Out of Court

At the core of the criminal justice process lie the courts—magistrates' courts, where nearly every adult criminal case starts out (and where the vast majority are concluded), youth courts for people below the age of 18, and the Crown Court, where more serious cases are tried by jury and the more serious offenders are sentenced by a judge.

The court arena is also a central focus for the probation service, for almost all its work comes, directly or indirectly, from this source. It is the courts which make probation orders and community service orders and which request pre-sentence reports (PSRs); it is the courts which pass prison sentences which lead to work before release and afterwards on parole or other forms of licence. In the civil justice system it is the family courts, at all levels, which require reports on residence and contact in relation to children. Probation officers have to learn to feel at home in court, to understand the processes, to play their part and to relate effectively with the other players in the administration of justice.

This is not simply a question of good relationships with magistrates and judges, although the confidence that sentencers have in their probation staff is vital to the smooth running of the court. There are other, equally important actors in the cast list for any court—the justices' clerk to whom the magistrates look for legal advice and the management of their daily business; barristers and solicitors who represent defendants; the Crown prosecutor who, as the name implies, prosecutes alleged offences; local news reporters; security staff who control access to the cells; and the court usher, usually a mine of useful information and with whom the court duty probation officer should always be on good terms.

A busy court looks, to those not centrally involved, like a particularly chaotic piece of unscripted and impromptu theatre. All too often bewildered defendants, bored or fearful spectators, police and other witnesses and WRVS tea ladies seem to be merely part of an endless stream of 'extras'. Making sure the court process works well requires considerable effort and the duty probation officer needs well honed skills of interviewing, background research and presentation.

Work starts well before the court and not all the work is undertaken by probation officers—a range of probation service officer grade staff (PSOs: see *Chapter 2*) also service the courts and bring a wealth of experience to this busy area of work.

COURT DUTY

First, court lists must be checked, to see where duty staff are most likely to be needed. Are there cases on which a pre-sentence report has previously been requested, and which must be presented today? Are there defendants, arrested overnight, who are already under supervision to probation colleagues? Are there cases in which a prison sentence or a remand in custody seems likely and a cell interview will have to be undertaken? These are the expected events and good planning will ensure that even a hard-pressed staff member can be in the right place at the right time. Expecting the unexpected, however, is where experience and planning will pay dividends.

Cases may be 'stood down' for a verbal report from the probation officer. This may be for some checking before a decision on bail or sentencing is made. It may be so that a brief interview can establish whether it is reasonable to pass sentence on the available information—or whether a more detailed, full PSR is required. This is pressurised work, often with few clues to go on.

• • •

Syed, aged 19, was a first offender, but had admitted an assault charge which the magistrates took very seriously, as he had inflicted head wounds with a bottle, following an incident at a mobile hamburger bar. Syed was indignant in court, rather than apologetic—he had been the victim of racist remarks and was not the initial aggressor. The probation officer used the 'stand-down' period to check with his college tutor, as well as to interview Syed and his sister, who had also come to court. The results were reassuring—his tutor described him as bright and intelligent and relating well to other students. He had completed two work placements in local factories without incident and might well get a job offer from one of the companies. Family issues were slightly more problematic—relationships with his elderly father were central—but his sister, who was 24 years of age, impressed as being very capable and active in her concerns. Syed was given a conditional discharge.

• • •

Martin, aged 28, had a string of minor offences, usually with gaps of up to 18 months between them, spread over the last 12 years. Theft, criminal damage and pub fights were most frequent, although drink driving was also there. He had, almost invariably, been fined and (a rarity, this) had always paid promptly. A single man with an impeccable work record, he was accompanied by his employer, who spoke for him in court and described him as 'the hardest worker I have ever known'. The Crown Court judge, who made it clear that he had been expecting to pass a prison sentence following a late guilty plea to an affray charge—a brawl in which some 30 young men had been involved—put the case back to the end of the day for the probation officer to interview. The brief written stand-down report described Martin as

> . . . a loner, with no real interests outside work and no social life except the pub. He would work seven days a week if he could – not for the money, but because it is what he enjoys most.

A community service order was suggested, and made. As expected, Martin completed it, flawlessly. After ten weeks of hard, physical work on a project constructing new facilities for a Riding for the Disabled scheme an astute community service officer decided to transfer him to the small band of carefully selected offenders who actually helped the disabled children and adults who benefited. Martin objected—a spade and a pickaxe were what he felt comfortable with. But he persevered, found other kinds of satisfaction despite his initial resistance, and stayed on to become a voluntary helper. It may not yet qualify as a social life but this, his first outside interest, provides social links and a feeling of worth on which he can build.

• • •

Carole, nicely dressed and well spoken, appeared on a second shoplifting charge. She insisted it was a momentary and forgetful lapse, that she would pay a fine and that all she wished was to 'get it over with'. She denied any problems and, in her mid-thirties, presented as a calm, contrite, organized person. This was a busy London court and the stipendiary magistrate (a salaried, full-time lawyer) saw dozens of apparently similar cases every day. He asked for a stand down report on the basis of a hunch, or momentary unease, and the probation officer, after taking the basic details, was unprepared for what followed.

'Was your husband not able to come to court with you today?' he asked.

Carole simply wept. It transpired that her husband was unaware of the hearing and that she had concealed the previous court appearance from him, too. She could hardly speak for sobbing, at first, then became more and more withdrawn. There were health, family and marriage

36

difficulties, it was clear—but no clear way of assessing them in a 40-minute interview like this.

The magistrate was given a brief, but guarded verbal report, asking for time to make a better assessment. He agreed to this, and asked for full reports three weeks later, so that the real work could begin.

• • •

The court duty officer will usually have to present PSRs, especially in cases like Carole's, above, where a colleague from a different service 50 miles away had to prepare the full report. Frank, an experienced officer, says this can often be a difficult task:

> When I joined the service . . . you nearly always went to the court with your own reports. That way, if there were any questions from the bench or the defending solicitor you could answer them directly. And you could use it to reinforce what you had said in the report—a few minutes in the witness box could be really persuasive. Now there simply isn't time to have three or four probation officers in court, waiting for their case to come up, so the duty officer has to do it all.

> That means good preparation—not just reading the report but trying to second-guess just what might come up . . . and trying to find the answers. The offender will know what is in the report, of course, but we have to give copies to the defence—and now the prosecutor, too. So there is plenty of scope for someone wanting to question it. I try to talk to the probation officer who wrote it, even if only for a couple of minutes. Sometimes you can get a "flavour" of the offender that even a first-class report can't quite manage—on paper. How well *can* you really explain a life on two sheets of A4?

Perhaps the hardest moments for court duty staff, whether in Magistrates' court or the Crown Court, come when someone is sentenced to custody. A cell interview is needed before they are taken off to prison and it has to be conducted regardless of other pressures and often in difficult circumstances. Offenders can be numb, fearful, angry (often at the probation officer whose report has, as they see it, failed them); they may have made no preparations for a sudden removal from home—pets, property, messages to friends and employers are suddenly uppermost in their minds—and family concerns are often equally vital. With the court still sitting 'upstairs', the duty officer has to coax, sympathise, be practical, not make promises that cannot be kept . . . and try and assess in some cases whether the offender is a suicide risk, so that the prison can be immediately informed.

Apart from work with individuals, the court duty officer needs to be able to answer more general questions about the policy of the local service or facilities which are available in the area; to record details of any cases in which reports have been requested or have been transferred to the Crown Court for trial; and to ensure that anyone in whom the probation service will have an interest—whether for a new report or an order—is seen before leaving court so that appointments can be made and obligations explained. Many defendants have little idea of what has actually been said to them in court; a careful explanation, 10 minutes later, when the anxiety and the confusion have lessened, is often needed to ensure that the next steps take place.

The Crown Court

Some special considerations affect work in the Crown Court, which has a distinct flavour, even though the principles remain the same. The Crown Court is usually staffed by a specialist unit—again, often a mix of probation officers and other staff—who aim to build up a working relationship with the resident judges and the greater number of recorders (part-time judges) and assistant recorders who may be sitting for only limited periods. With a range of much more serious offences than those tried in the magistrates' court, prison sentences are much more common and because offences are generally more serious any recommendation for probation or community service is likely to come under greater scrutiny.

Other general considerations

Court probation staff must be well informed about special programmes (for drug treatment or for sex offenders, for instance); realistic about risks and seriousness; honest about the limitations of what the probation service can offer and quick to understand the key factors which might help a court reach a decision.

If they can do so, court staff at all levels can fulfil their function as the 'eyes and ears' of the sentencer. Building up trust, retaining an independent standpoint and taking a realistic view are the basis of mutual respect. Once established, the court will often be prepared to take calculated risks on the basis of the duty officer's assessment.

Court work provides a never ending set of challenges, drama, pressure and variety for the staff who represent the service there. The professionals who attend regularly soon get to recognise each other's ways of working and there are dangers in it becoming a mutually supportive 'club' which pays rather less regard to defendants, witnesses and others who have no such familiarity. Once that balance has been properly established, however, it can be a very satisfying area of work and the skills it develops are easily transferable into other areas of probation work.

BAIL INFORMATION SCHEMES

An important development in recent years has been the development of bail information schemes. These aim to provide verified information to the Crown prosecutor (with a copy to the defence) so that courts can make better informed decisions on whether a defendant should be remanded on bail or in custody. There are some important issues here, of justice (for the defendant will not necessarily be found guilty); of risk (because of concerns about continued offending on bail); and, of course, money plays a part since the cost of prison places (a significant proportion of which are taken up by remand prisoners) is one of the many pressures on a beleaguered prison service.

Two kinds of Bail Information Schemes exist; one, court-based (a 'first remand' scheme) and the other prison-based (a 'second remand' scheme). For convenience, both are dealt with here since the court remains the decision making body and the *National Standards for Bail Information Schemes* (Home Office: 1995) cover both. At court, schemes are operated by the probation service; prison schemes use a mix of prison and probation staff.

Court-based schemes
In court schemes, a probation service staff member visits the court early for cell interviews, armed with details of charges, previous convictions and police objections to bail. Information about defendants who may be mentally disordered or otherwise vulnerable is quickly gained and a priority list established, for in busy urban courts it will rarely be possible to see everyone. The bail information officer explains the purpose of the interview and, with the consent of the defendant, looks at issues which are likely to be at the heart of the court's decision. Is there a suitable address for the defendant to go to and, if not, can one be found? Will this mean application to a hostel? Are there risks to the public or to the welfare of children which have been identified? Does the defendant have work to which he or she can return? Enough time has to be left for these to be verified and a short written report prepared before the court hears the application, so deadlines are always important.

Prison-based schemes

In prison-based schemes, work begins only when a remand in custody has been ordered at the first hearing, so additional information on why the court refused bail is also available. Such schemes are clearly second-best in the sense that an earlier decision might have been able to avoid custody at all, but they may be the only practical alternative when covering a large number of smaller courts. The remand prison, covering a wide area, may be the only cost effective way of reaching enough defendants to make a scheme possible.

Prison-based schemes do have advantages, too. Information has to be available for the second court hearing, which usually gives a week for any information to be checked, and any plans made. It means that difficult hostel placements are more likely to be successfully negotiated, alternative bail addresses found and extra interviews arranged in cases where the court-based 'same-day' schemes would have faced an impossible task. The best prison-based schemes may lead to bail in up to 40 per cent of the cases where reports are made to the courts—a very cost effective outcome. (This should not obscure the fact that a significant proportion of remand prisoners choose not to co-operate—some because they recognise their offence is so serious that prison is inevitable, some because prison is preferable to what may be outside. By way of example, the Kent scheme, based on three remand prisons but covering all the courts in the county saw 648 'eligible' prisoners during 1996-97. Of these, 439 had reports submitted for a second hearing, and 181 were bailed as a result.

PRE-SENTENCE REPORTS

The pre-sentence report (PSR) is the 'shop window' of the probation service and the perception of the service by sentencers at all levels is largely shaped by the quality and relevance of this single document. The report is there to help the court in determining the most suitable method of dealing with the offender and, in an arena that encourages partisan views, it has to be impartial, balanced and factually accurate. In, usually, a page and a half of text it has to provide an assessment of the nature and causes of someone's offending behaviour and the action which might be most effective in stopping or reducing reoffending.

If a PSR is to be really useful it has to make the offender 'come alive'—to be understandable in the context of the whole of their life and not just the few minutes of behaviour which has led to them being placed in the dock. Good report writing is an invaluable skill and the process of improving technique—whether through practice or training—is likely to be continuous.

National Standards requirements for pre-sentence reports take up more space than is allocated to any single community penalty—a recognition of the key role they play in both decision-making in court and in determining the work of the service. After certain standard information, including a note of the sources of information which have been used to prepare the report, the PSR is set out under the following headings:

- Introduction
- Offence analysis
- Relevant information about the offender
- Risk to the public of reoffending
- Conclusion.

The key to *offence analysis* lies in the second word. Reports are prepared after conviction, or when it is known that a guilty plea will be entered. Courts must ordinarily obtain such reports after conviction and before deciding whether to impose custody or any of the more enhanced forms of community sentence, although since 1994 they have had a discretion to dispense with a PSR where they deem one to be unnecessary. Most courts seem to consider a PSR to be good practice in virtually all cases where a community sentence or imprisonment appears to be a possibility, and are reluctant to presume that a report is uneccesary. The court will already have a factual description of events from the Crown prosecutor but many of the questions crucial to an understanding of what went on are likely to remain unanswered. What is the offender's explanation? Does he or she accept responsibility, show remorse, appreciate the effect on the victim? Were problems of drug or alcohol misuse a factor? And what about unemployment, personal, medical or psychiatric problems? Is this a single incident or part of a pattern of behaviour and is there evidence of serious risk of harm to the public?

Understanding the offence—or at least seeing it in context—inevitably leads to a clearer picture of the offender. The following report was written on a 31 year old man, Stephen Williams, who had admitted causing £800 of damage to a neon sign and shop window at a local department store. The offence was ten months old by the time it came to court and a good deal had happened in the interim period:

Introduction
In preparing this report I have interviewed Mr Williams at both his home and in the office. I have also interviewed his girl friend, Stella South and

her parents with whom he is now living; and Mrs Ann Street, who currently employs him. I have had access to Crown Prosecution Service papers and to previous probation service records in London and Devon.

Offence analysis

The offence was committed in the late autumn of last year—now nearly 10 months ago. Mr Williams was sleeping rough at the time, and using the shop doorway as an overnight shelter. He says he has only the haziest of recollections of the offence and was so drunk that, even when released from the police station later that night, he was unaware that he faced court proceedings. He awoke the following day without any paperwork and assumed he had been cautioned. He decided, in line with his usual pattern to move on to another town where the police did not know him. This explains his failure to appear in court and the length of time before these proceedings. He accepts that he must take responsibility for the offence and is glumly realistic about the prospect of substantial compensation payments.

Relevant information about the offender

The offence has to be seen in the context of his lifestyle at the date of its commission and the very real changes which have taken place since then. Briefly, his background includes a childhood spent partly in care and partly with foster-parents; a series of short term relationships and a long history of offending, much of it alcohol-related theft and criminal damage. He served nine prison sentences between 1984 and 1996 and the usual pattern is of release to hostel accommodation, short term co-operation while being supervised on licence—and periods of freedom which rarely lasted more than a few months.

He was last released from prison in August 1995. His wife had ended their marriage while he was in prison and he survived the next year living with friends, in squats, or in a tent. He took casual work when he could find it and enjoyed a good reputation as a hard worker when the work appealed. When the fruit picking season ended and winter approached he quickly reverted to the aimless pattern which culminated in this offence. I would not assess him as an alcoholic; he drinks only occasionally when working, but heavily when bored, depressed, angry or frustrated. Since these four conditions accurately sum up his life at the time the offence occurred, the end product was fairly predictable.

The turning point came earlier this year when he was begging in the High Street. A lady stopped and asked: 'Can you use a spade?' Surprised, he answered yes and she said: 'Well, get up then, because I have got work for you'. His new employer, Mrs Ann Street, gave him casual gardening work and, once satisfied about his reliability, then sought additional work from other members of her church congregation. He now has three or four days work a week; earns about £100 per week gross and is slowly building a sustainable pattern as a self-employed gardener.

Three months ago he met Stella South, who is aged 25. After a short period living together the couple moved in to live with Ms South's parents. They have proved very supportive and will continue to provide accommodation in return for some work until Mr Williams and Stella can explore other options. They hope to obtain a live-in position offering domestic/gardening work and have already been interviewed for two such posts.

Risk to the public of reoffending

Virtually all his offending in the last few years has been linked to alcohol misuse, lack of proper accommodation or lack of any stable relationship. Any combination of these makes the risk of reoffending high but, equally, his current situation reduces any risk substantially as long as progress can be sustained. his position is probably more stable and more hopeful than at any time in the last decade.

Conclusion

Some of these changes are, as yet, very short term but he has a fierce pride, a truculent intelligence and an appetite for hard work which suggest that he could make good use of any help which was offered. He has said that he would be keen to co-operate in any period of supervision, if offered by the court and both Stella and her mother have indicated that they would welcome additional support while the progress of the last six months can be reinforced and sustained. The most suitable sentence, which offers the best way of reducing the risk of reoffending would—I think—be a probation order. It would aim to:

- concentrate on practical goals in relation to the payment of compensation, employment and accommodation. Interviews for 'live in' posts tend to finish when he reveals his criminal record. Help from our Employment Team may be crucial in this area
- provide an outside 'safety net' when the inevitable difficulties occur. The South family have started this process—and helped him to stop drinking—but recognise how much more needs to be done
- work with him on an individual basis. Contact would be at least weekly during the first three months of the order, with referral to an 'alcohol and offending' group if appropriate

If the court were prepared to consider such a course I believe a 12 month period would be appropriate. A fine seems unrealistic given his likely liability in terms of compensation; and a community service order, whilst well within his capacity, would not address the real issues which he now has to face.

Andrew Headland
Probation Officer

The key to this unusual story was to help the court see the offence in a *new* context, rather than the depressing litany of failure to which his string of previous convictions bore witness. Courts are surprisingly ready to give offenders a second (or third, or sixth) chance—but only if circumstances really do seem to warrant it and a well-planned pattern of supervision can be seen to reduce the risk of further trouble. In the event, Mrs Street, whose surprise offer of work was the real turning point, came to court to argue for Stephen and the court, both surprised and impressed, made a probation order.

It seemed to the probation officer that, while a collection of gardening jobs would be sufficient during the summer, Stephen and Stella needed to plan ahead for the time when regular work dried up. The probation service Employment Team were clear that being open about Stephen's criminal record was essential—but recognised that it might well make the possibility of live-in work unrealistic.

Supervision had its ups and downs, with an occasional crisis call when frustration turned to despair (and, twice, to memorable binges and equally memorable and contrite hangovers). But Stella, whose interest in gardening had been the starting point for their relationship did not give up easily. Eventually, both secured places on a horticulture course at a local college; and are now looking at a longer-term future and will be able to take a recognised qualification (as well as a long record) to job interviews. In the meantime, weekend and holiday gardening work with Stephen's original customers keeps them solvent.

Quality a priority

Improving the quality of pre-sentence reports has been a national priority for some time, with two joint inspections between the Probation Inspectorate and the Association of Chief Probation Officers (ACOP). This search for constant improvement is hardly surprising; the purpose of the PSR

> to provide a professional assessment of the nature and causes of a person's offending behaviour and the action which can be taken to reduce reoffending

is at the very heart of the probation service's role. Particular care has to be taken with assessments of whether the current offence seems to conform to a pattern of previous offending; the offender's capacity for change; whether previous community sentences have produced a positive response; and whether it is possible to analyse the risk of further offending—for instance if the offence was racially motivated.

Clarity of language and avoiding jargon are equally important if the credibility of the report is to be maintained. Most probation services have quality control, or 'gatekeeping' systems to try and ensure that inaccuracies and discriminatory language or jargon are removed—but stories of particularly choice examples (some, I suspect, going back for decades) will always be quoted. 'This nuclear family is multi-delinquent, with a high incarceration index' (all his brothers are in prison); and 'He has a negative response to interactive relationships' (he cannot get on with his probation officer), serve only as Awful Warnings to new probation officers. But perhaps that is still a useful function.

The PSR's conclusion: A note

The conclusion of any report should flow, seamlessly, from the information contained in the previous sections but it is here that the delicate balance between the probation officer (whose prime task is to assess what might be best for the individual) and the court (who have to represent the whole community) becomes crucial. The probation officer is expected to make a *proposal*, not a *recommendation* and whilst this may seem mere sophistry there is, in that difference, a recognition of the authority of the court, and its role as the decision-maker, remains central.

Proposals should reflect the seriousness of the offence, the impact any specific proposal might have on offending behaviour and—if a period of supervision is proposed—a clear supervision plan. David was a 27 year old, in court for offences of begging and possessing cannabis. He had outstanding fines in half a dozen other courts, lived in a squat with others whose lifestyle meant further offences were likely—and recognised that he was just about at rock bottom. He saw his own problems as centring on his lack of literacy—because job applications, tenancy agreements and many other aspects of everyday life were beyond him. But the PSR writer recognised that a one track approach would fail. She wrote in her conclusion, having proposed a probation order:

Some intensive contact would be needed over a relatively short period, with the following programme:

- practical help in relation to accommodation
- attendance at the Drug Advice Centre programme. The probation service would also maintain close links with staff there
- specialist help from our employment officer, which would focus on pre-work training and literacy, rather than immediate work
- work on an individual basis in terms of help with relationships; and
- support in moving away from his current life-style.

And the court accepted this as a realistic programme if supervision was to have a real chance of success.

Not all reports, of course, will be able to suggest the positive programmes which the previous cases warranted—sometimes because the seriousness of the offence means that a prison sentence is inevitable, sometimes because a period of probation supervision would be unlikely to offer any realistic chance of reducing the risk of reoffending. The following cases examine the way in which probation officers' recommendations in pre-sentence reports can still be helpful to the courts.

CASE STUDIES

Edward Wiltshire

Edward was 37, and appeared on two counts of falsely claiming social security benefits. He had not been in trouble for ten years, at which time a charge of dishonesty (retaining passenger fares) had cost him his job as a railway guard. Two previous convictions, at the age of 19, were recorded, but not felt to be really relevant. The current offences sprang directly from acute financial pressures of an unusual kind.

Over two years earlier, he had participated in a 'big card game' in order to try and make money. He had had to give up work as a roofer because of medical problems with his balance and, while he had saved a few hundred pounds, he was facing unemployment and some hardship.

Naively, he took £200 to the game, saying he '. . . used to be good at cards' and thought he could win. Losses of £1,000 proved a shock and, in an attempt to right the situation, he ended with debts of £5,000 in games that were almost certainly rigged. Within weeks he was getting phone calls threatening violence if he did not pay his debts; soon, he was handing over his entire two-weekly unemployment benefit cheque of £190. His wife was furious and though she began to work full time the strain—both financial and matrimonial—was enormous. It led to a short separation and during this time, his creditors visited his wife and family to reinforce the threats to them, too, if payments were not continued.

By the time the matter came to court he had found new work on a construction site and the gambling debt had, painfully, been paid. The PSR concluded that gambling was no longer a significant factor in his life—a painfully learned lesson; that his wife now organized all their joint finances; that family strengths were such that further offending seemed unlikely and that repayments of fraudulently obtained benefit, albeit small, had already begun. A community service order was suggested as an appropriate penalty, and ordered by the court.

Joanne Couples

At age 26, Joanne had also tried to resolve outstanding debts by turning to crime. She agreed to act as a drugs courier but was arrested on her first trip and, with over £80,000 worth of heroin in her possession, and knew that her plea of guilty would result in a prison sentence. The pre-sentence report, undertaken in a series of interviews in the remand prison, could nevertheless pass on much useful information.

Joanne had a disturbed and difficult background, much of it spent in children's homes and foster parent placements, from which she often ran away. It was a particularly chaotic adolescence, with little formal schooling; although clearly intelligent, her literacy was poor and undermined what little self-confidence she had. There had been good periods, usually associated with living-in jobs in hotels and bad ones when, while dependent on drugs, she had been abused and exploited by the men with whom she had short term relationships.

Four months on remand had cleared her mind and her body, too, had begun to recover from years of neglect. She had refused to see any of her old associates and, having been told to expect a six year prison sentence, was planning eventually to create a new life. Much of the interviews with the probation officer were focused on this and the final section of the report to the Crown Court read as follows.

Joanne recognises that a prison sentence is inevitable and deserved. Her acceptance of this, and her determination to start completely afresh on her eventual release are impressive. She has already benefited considerably from medical help and attendance at a voluntary drugs group. She has now started work on her literacy problems and aims, realistically, to complete her education at this late stage. Both prison staff and myself have been impressed by her determination and her potential, and sentence planning will aim to

— explore vocational training opportunities for the future
— consolidate links with the probation service in the area to which she will move in due course
— make realistic plans for accommodation and employment help on release and for sustaining support and help in what will still be a difficult period.

To this end, a probation volunteer worker is already in touch and will stay involved throughout the sentence.

I assess the risk of reoffending as very low. The shorter the period of custody, the sooner she can make the very real contribution to the

47

community of which she is capable. This was a disastrous, as well as an incompetent, episode. She has learnt from it.

Joanne received a three year sentence, the judge commenting that it was the shortest term he could impose, consistent with his wider public duty. With the long period spent on remand, it meant that, within six months, Joanne was released early on licence and was ready to start afresh. Nor has she ever looked back.

Peter Kurley

At 22, Peter was in court for the eighth time. A series of offences of criminal damage (£1,500 of damage to parked cars) and theft (of two mopeds) were, once again, linked to his drinking. Sober, he was a delight—intelligent, responsive, articulate and full of good intentions. Magistrates found it difficult to believe that he could be the same person described in prosecution evidence. But when drunk, which was often, he was violent, foul-mouthed, alarmingly anti-social and recklessly criminal.

His solicitor dwelt at some length on a difficult family background and an injury which had made him abandon his chosen career. A short marriage, followed by a bitter parting, had made things worse. A last chance, with specialist alcohol treatment was the priority. The PSR report took a less sanguine view.

> He has been on probation three times. All these orders were unsuccessful and were terminated early because of a new offence. Similarly, on the one occasion on which a community service order was made he completed 40 hours to a high standard; then his attendance and the quality of his work became much more erratic. He was warned, then faced breach proceedings which coincided with another offence.
>
> Residential treatment has been tried, as a condition of a probation order but he walked out after three weeks. I asked him to attend the local addictions centre during the remand period but he did so only once, briefly, before making publicly offensive remarks and leaving. It is quite unrealistic to suggest that any community penalty will have any effect while he is so unmotivated and resistant to help. His good intentions evaporate almost before they form. I have no constructive options to offer the court which might help reduce the risk of reoffending.

Realistic, credible reports are the basis of mutual respect and trust between courts and probation officers. It will not exist for long if PSRs are simply seen to be mitigation for the offender, or a supplementary plea for the defence. Nor can proposals in reports always be expected to be followed—about one in four make suggestions (usually for community penalties) which the court feels unable to accept. Sentencers have a difficult task in weighing the needs of society against those of the individual offender. Those needs frequently conflict and both magistrates and judges are often pilloried for decisions they make which try to accommodate both. Trust in the judgement of probation staff who prepare reports and advise courts is a key element in the quality of sentencing decisions. Some 224,000 PSRs were prepared for courts in 1996, with a further 30,000 reports focusing on specific enquiries (bail enquiries, or in connection with unpaid fines). It represents some of the most important and public work undertaken by probation staff and report writing skills are necessarily important in selection and recruitment decisions.

THE BASIS OF THE COURT'S DECISION

It is not appropriate in a non-technical handbook to provide detailed information about sentencing. But it is important to note that all information provided to courts by way of a PSR or otherwise occurs against the background of the statutory sentencing framework introduced by the Criminal Justice Act 1991 (as later amended). That framework as set out in *The Sentence of the Court* is reproduced in *Appendix V* at p. 167. Certain key points should be noted:

- there are threshold tests for the different levels of sentence and, in particular, statutory criteria for:
  —*community sentences:* the offence under consideration (or that offence and other associated offences) must be *serious enough* to merit such a sentence; the restriction of liberty created by the sentence must be commensurate with the seriousness of the offence(s); and the community order or orders selected must be the most suitable for the offender
  —*custody:* The offence must be so serious that *only* such a sentence can be justified; or, if the offence is a sexual or violent offence (both as defined by the 1991 Act), 'only such a sentence would be adequate to protect the public from serious harm' from the offender. Custody is also possible where the offender has refused to consent to one of the few types of community sentence still requiring such consent (below); and on breach of certain community sentences following 'wilful and persistent' failure to comply. The length of a custodial sentence must be commensurate with the seriousness of the offence(s) or, as appropriate, the need to protect the public from serious harm from a sexual or violent offender.

49

- before deciding upon sentence, a court must take into account all information available to it regarding the seriousness of the *offence(s)*, including any *aggravating* or *mitigating* factors; similarly all information concerning the *offender* where the protection of the public criterion is under consideration
- this includes information contained in a PSR, which must be obtained and considered by the court before most of the more demanding forms of community sentence, or custody, are ordered. Although there is now a power for the court to dispense with a PSR where it deems one to be unnecessary, good practice means that courts still generally request reports in such circumstances. There is, in any event, in relation to community service, a separate requirement for a court to be satisfied that the offender is a suitable person to perform work under the order and that work is available (a 'community service assessment'). Unlike a PSR this assessment can be oral or written (in practice it is usually in writing and often incorporated into the PSR)
- some courts give provisional, non-binding indications of seriousness when calling for a PSR, or mention items of particular concern to assist the PSR writer
- since 1997, the offender's consent is not required to a community sentence, except in relation to probation conditions concerning treatment for a mental condition or drug/alcohol dependency. Both of these require an expression of 'willingness to comply'. Nonetheless, willingness/motivation may be a relevant issue for the PSR writer as part of his or her more general analysis
- whether to make a compensation order in favour of a victim of crime (and any voluntary reparation or amends made by the offender) is always a material consideration and a factor in the court's overall decision.

CHAPTER 4

On Probation

Neil, aged 27, was before the Crown Court for four burglaries of office and factory premises, with a total value of £7,000. Three other offences would also be taken into consideration. His criminal history went back 12 years, with 16 previous convictions including two in the previous two years. He had already been in prison seven times and was glumly expecting the worst. 'This'll be the big'un', he said, speculating on his likely future, 'because I've only been out eight months, see'.

Yet Neil, who came from a large family and had grown up in a very delinquent city estate, did not fit the pattern which the probation officer who met him to prepare the pre-sentence report (PSR), had in mind. Neil had been well known to the city centre probation team over the years but had moved recently to a housing association tenancy in Heatherlands, a development in a village some five miles from the city. He had married three years ago and there were two children, aged three and one on whom he clearly doted. His wife, Deirdre, was in despair at his behaviour and was equally distraught at the thought of having to cope on her own. She thought they might have to give up the house and return to her mother in a cramped city flat—not just because of the money, but for support, too. Yet this was exactly the environment in which Neil had grown up, and grown into trouble, like most of his family. And it was his recognition that he had to get away to change, that had led to the couple's move.

The first interview at the office had convinced Maurice Peters, the probation officer, that Neil was at a crucial stage. None of his offences had ever been committed on his own—he had always been 'one of the gang' and welcomed by older boys because of his sharp mind and lively approach. Neil could always spot a good way in to a darkened factory, or know instinctively the line of retreat if the alarm should sound, and he was much in demand. Even the inevitable captures and court appearances were a kind of bonding and, as the youngest, he often got the lightest sentence. There was something about him, not least an intelligent and enquiring mind, that appealed to sentencers as well.

Two earlier spells on probation had been full of good intentions, with Neil agreeing enthusiastically to attendance at adventure courses (as an 18 year old) and social skills groupwork programmes (when he was 22). Neither order lasted the two year course that was intended— each time the good intentions evaporated when Neil was sucked back

51

into group offences. Much the same happened on a 180-hour community service order, when Neil completed almost three quarters of the hours to a very high standard . . . then, in his own words '. . . blew it all, one Friday night for a few miserable quid'.

Everyone agreed that unemployment and the lack of a decent income was the major problem. Neil himself pointed out that the move to Heatherlands had been expensive, let alone the money that had to be spent on the children. And being five miles away meant work was even more difficult to find and that it was even more expensive for Deirdre and the children to visit parents and family. Neil's work record was almost non-existent, although it was clear that lots of casual work at various times had never reached official records, and had kept him solvent between prison sentences. In his part of the North-East either leaving school with a poor record; or coming from one or two well known estates; or having a criminal record, would automatically make your chances of finding a job remote indeed. Neil had all three hurdles to overcome. He had soon stopped trying and now, ten years on, had nothing to offer except weeks here and there on demolition sites and new housing projects, a few weeks ('In charge!' he said, as if still shocked) at a pre-Christmas shoppers car park, and a lot of wasted years.

Deirdre had been the spur to do better, as had been the birth of his first child. But he began to despair when nothing changed, when debts mounted, when the pressures of his new family commitments suddenly seemed a millstone. He promised himself it would be 'just one job' and at first, it was. His £300 from the shareout after a burglary kept his and Deirdre's heads above water and, although Deirdre hated it, two subsequent 'nights out' followed as he got drawn back into crime. Now, however, he was one of the oldest of the group and the 12 month sentence which followed the inevitable arrest meant he missed the birth of his second child.

Moving away from their families was a wrench—but it was also a chance to begin again when Neil left prison. The new house offered everything he and Deirdre had ever wanted. It also sucked them straight back into greater debt. This time Neil would not even tell his wife that he was returning to crime and his arrest, for stealing goods from a council storage depot, came as an ever greater shock.

Maurice admitted that he 'pushed Neil hard' in that first interview. Why should any court want to keep him out of prison? Wasn't he just a repeat offender, with whom nothing worked? Would his marriage survive another period in prison, and how would his children react to an absent Dad? Other people got jobs—why not him?

'He was almost incoherent with desperation and fear', Maurice said later. 'The fear that what little he had he would lose; the desperation that he would step back into a hopeless future and that he was helpless to stop it'. Maurice agreed to see Deirdre before a final interview with Neil. He returned from the home visit enormously impressed with the effort and love that the couple had put into their home and family but equally depressed by the picture that also emerged. Deirdre agreed that she was a 'bad manager' and money didn't seem to go anywhere. She knew the pressure this put on Neil, but looking after two small children and not being able to make ends meet had ground her slowly down— depressed and tearful and, above all, tired. Family support was always there, but somehow even the days when her Mum came out to look after the children (bringing as many treats as she could afford) only left her with an even deeper sense of failure. Now Neil was angry because she had no time for him . . . and she knew that sooner or later, like so many of her friends, she would be left to cope alone.

Maurice Peters talked long and hard to colleagues before his final interview with Neil. 'The more he thought about court, the more apathy took over', said Maurice. 'I had to stir him into believing that he could actually achieve something if he *did* get a chance. When he told me he didn't think he'd get probation because he'd let us down before, I let rip. 'D'you not think you let *yourself* down? I shouted at him; 'D'you not want to do something for yourself and your family? I got enough of a response to convince me it was now or never and I decided I would go to court with him, because I knew the odds were poor'.

The report to the Crown Court proposed a combination order— probation and community service combined in the most demanding sentence, short of custody, that could be devised. The report was realistic about the risk of reoffending but proposed a five pronged programme to reduce those risks and to build something more positive for the future

The community service, as well as being a simple 'paying back' would test out his capacity and willingness to work straight away. As long as he was unemployed, he would undertake two whole-day sessions each week

Probation would involve some intensive work in the first three months:

— help from the service's employment officer, who would assess realistically what might be possible for Neil
— individual sessions both in the office and at home, so that Deirdre could be part of ongoing planning and work

— a six week 'Drinkers Group' run by a local voluntary body. It was clear that sporadic bouts of drinking were Neil's refuge when problems mounted, and that they were closely linked with his offending; and

— a volunteer would see both Neil and Deirdre to help them with budgeting and managing the household finances.

Neil left the court with a two year combination order, including 100 hours (the maximum) of community service and a stern lecture from the Crown Court judge, who made it clear that he wanted three month and six month progress reports and that any breach of the order would mean a substantial prison sentence.

Maurice had prepared for the order, despite doubts about whether Neil would be allowed his freedom. 'He was in court on Friday, our usual day for guilty pleas', he said, 'and I was determined he should see just how serious I was in making him keep his contract with the court. He started his community service the next day, *and* on the Sunday— two different projects, but I wanted to see how he would react—and he had to see me on Monday for a long interview so we could start his supervision plan'.

It was uphill work, although Neil soon demonstrated that he would do well on community service. He liked the work—painting a community centre on Saturday, helping to restore a wheelchair path at a country park on Sunday—and worked cheerfully and hard. But he was more resistant to individual work, whether alone or with Deirdre. He was scornful of the Alcohol Group ('like going back to school') and denied that he had a problem; was completely unrealistic in his expectations of Jill, the employment officer; and resentful of Pam Bowles, the volunteer who had agreed to help the couple. After three months it was clear that it was Deirdre who had made the best use of Pam, and that Pam's steady support, practical help and interest and non-judgemental approach were helping Deirdre to believe they could succeed. Neil himself was mostly meeting the various requirements of the combination order but, it seemed, giving very little. He missed the last session of the Alcohol Group, and an office appointment and Maurice had to warn him and confirm in writing that a return to court for not complying with the order would follow if there were any other failures.

By this time Neil had finished his community service hours. For the last four weeks his supervisor, impressed both by his attitude and a natural sympathy for children, had placed him in a residential home for children and young adults with learning difficulties. In between very practical work he helped staff with the residents and his mixture of quiet determination in helping them with simple tasks and endless patience as they re-learned them meant that they regarded him as far more than an 'ordinary' offender on placement. Neil had quickly formed a special bond with a very withdrawn youngster and agreed to continue seeing him on a voluntary basis; staff soon asked if he would undertake some sessional work. The inevitable difficulties over police checks before employment meant that Maurice and Jill had to be involved—not just in confirming the previous offences he had disclosed, but in providing extra information and assessments of his potential.

Neil later agreed that this had been the turning point—that probation staff whom he had seen as 'controlling' or organizing him had not just worked hard to help him—but had tangible faith in his ability to change. Sessions became less frequent, but much more productive as Neil's defences slipped—they worked together to understand how and when the danger of a relapse into drink or offending might occur; and how to change the previous pattern. Home visits, in some of which Pam Bowles was also involved, helped the couple to devise joint plans and to realise how they could help each other.

It took ten months before Neil could move from occasional sessional work to a full time post in the residential home. Sleeping-in duties were, he wryly admitted 'good for cash but bad for family life', but adjustments were soon made and, four months later, Maurice successfully applied for his order to be discharged for good progress.

Neil's summing-up of the period of supervision was that 'He [the probation officer] helped me grow up'. But behind that simple truth lay, first, some dogged and persistent work with a suspicious and resentful young man; then, some skilled and creative work from a variety of people to use the growing motivation and acceptance on offer. It was, as Maurice pointed out, a team effort.

• • •

Neil's case illustrates some of the day-to-day work which goes on in relation to many probation orders. It also demonstrates some of the tensions inherent in holding several different roles:

- *An officer of the court* Maurice had to ensure that the contract with the Court was properly kept and in having to warn Neil that Breach action would be taken when two appointments had been missed he was reinforcing the authority inherent in this role.

- *A case manager* Maurice needed to keep the various components of the order, whether delivered by a colleague (community service), a volunteer (family contact) or another agency (the alcohol group) in some sort of balance. Simply adding more elements to the order may not be helpful—the demands may just be too great. Maurice needed to pace those demands to ensure that Neil could not only meet them, but benefit

- *A case worker* Within the overall case management Maurice still had a key role as a social worker. Individual counselling and help were needed at different times in varying amounts; they were the cement which kept the other elements in place, and the role of the probation officer remains a fascinating amalgam of all three.

The balance will depend not only on individual cases, but on the way individual probation services are organized, and on the emerging political context.

Service organization—partly a matter of choice, or budget pressures or geography—will see probation officers in some areas move much more extensively to a case management model, where oversight of the order, regular reviews and risk assessment are the main responsibilities. In this model, increasing amounts of face-to-face work, whether in groups, on a one-to-one basis or in reporting centres in the latter stage of the order will be undertaken by specialist staff. This may be because it is more cost effective, or because more consistent programmes can be run by using specialists—but the old notion of a single probation officer meeting all the needs within an order has long since gone.

'Advise, assist and befriend'—the original statement of purpose from the Probation of First Offenders Act 1907 (see *Chapter 1*)—still holds a central truth, but its application does not depend on a single relationship with an individual probation officer. One probation officer—the case manager—may hold continuity but will not be the only significant individual for the offender. This shift has not been easy, although the evidence has been available for a long time. As early as the 1960s in a Home Office study of the Middlesex Probation Area it was shown that, far from being disadvantaged by having more than one probation officer during the course of the order, many offenders enjoyed the chance of a change, responded well to a new face, and outcomes could be better.

The political context will also have some impact although not always the ones politicians expect. The early 1990s, with its emphasis on severity of punishment, the language of the 'War Against Crime', and the drive towards more social control brought significant additional pressures to managers and probation officers alike. It was a change which emphasised personal freedom and individual responsibility—but tended to discount the influence of social and family situations and circumstance. Whatever the political rhetoric, however, it is in communities that the probation service has its identity and strength and it is in communities that effective means of dealing with criminality are to be found. The tensions which resulted led to sustained criticism of probation as a 'soft option' and concerted attempts to 'toughen-up' the conditions applying to all community sentences.

Probation and its delivery

The statutory purposes of probation remain:

- to secure the rehabilitation of the offender
- to protect the public from serious harm from the offender or to prevent the commission by him or her of further offences

and within this framework there is considerable scope for discretion, for helping, coaxing and cajoling offenders through their order, despite difficulties and crises, and for demanding compliance with the conditions set by the court where that is needed.

Interestingly, as the mechanisms of control become more apparent, so probation may find its own role develops more clearly. One of the findings with electronic tagging has been the realisation that, although the tag seems to be effective for only short periods, it may 'buy time' for other longer lasting programmes to take effect. Joint orders—an electronically tagged curfew with a probation order, for instance, have been surprisingly effective with difficult drug offenders and the scope for this parallel approach may be considerable.

Probation orders do not work merely because an hour or so of time each week is used as a reminder of the original offence and the penalty imposed. They work because of the way individual motivation can be harnessed and because of the quality of input from probation and other staff.

Having someone in authority question you about your life, your attitudes and beliefs, your actions, hopes and fears, is very intrusive and it may take time before it becomes effective. Offenders go through different stages—sullen compliance, polite co-operation, anger, challenge, withdrawal and aggression are all common enough—before the two-way nature of the contract begins to be relevant to them. For some, a wary cooperation may be all that can be achieved; others may suddenly realise that the understanding someone else has achieved can be even more powerfully realised by themselves.

The 'standard' probation order may be from six months to three years in length and all orders contain conditions requiring the offender to:

- be under the supervision of a probation officer
- keep in touch as instructed and receive home visits
- inform the supervising officer of any change of address or employment
- be of good behaviour and lead an industrious life.

These are sometimes called 'standard conditions'. Within this framework National Standards make quite specific demands. The initial meeting between supervising officer and offender has to take place within five days of the making of the order and should cover, clearly and in detail, what is expected of the offender and what he or she can expect from the probation service. A written *supervision plan* which will be regularly reviewed, has to be drawn up within ten days and must cover problems, needs, the risk of reoffending or serious harm to the public; work to be done to make the offender aware of the impact of their crimes, especially on victims; an individual programme and timescale for the objectives set. (A summary of National Standards is given in *Appendix III*).

Probation plus
Standard conditions—which, in reality, can be very demanding—may be all that is needed. But there is scope for a wide range of additional conditions. They may be imposed to increase the restriction of liberty, to deal with a specific problem or to recognise the seriousness of the offence and they are increasingly used by courts. They may be:

- *a requirement as to residence* in a hostel, approved lodgings or as directed by the probation officer
- *a requirement for probation centre attendance or on a 'specified activities' programme* These intensive programmes are used for more serious offenders
- *a requirement to receive psychiatric treatment* This can only be used when the court has an assessment from a psychiatrist and when treatment is actually available
- *a requirement to receive treatment for drug or alcohol dependency.*

Courts have a general discretion to impose other requirements to meet special needs within the overall purpose of a probation or combination order.

Within these additional requirements a wide variety of special programmes have been developed. Examples include the following:

- *Offending behaviour group* An 18-week session covering problem solving skills and techniques, helping offenders recognise high risk situations—and to deal with them; victim issues; and understanding and managing emotions, especially anger
- *Auto offenders group* The aim is to challenge attitudes and behaviour which lead to auto offending, to encourage legal and responsible driving and to educate and inform in the areas of safe driving, road use and motoring law.
- *Burglars group* This pays particular attention to the impact on victims, challenges attitudes and behaviour and applies more general strategies to try and reduce offending.

Learning within a group can often be much more effective than through individual sessions and we shall consider the implications later. The main use of additional programmes, however, comes in relation to the two single most common factors in offending—drink and drugs.

DEALING WITH DRINK AND DRUGS

Crime has strong links with alcohol and drug misuse. Research suggests that 41 per cent of people on probation had committed offences to support their addictions and that a quarter of *all* those in contact with the service—around 50,000 people—were serious drug misusers. At local level, a survey in Dorset showed that 46 per cent of those on community orders had drink problems and 35 per cent had drug problems; in Suffolk, for people released from prison in 1996 the figures were 46 per cent and 55 per cent. Of equal significance, a study over a six year period in Kent showed that while the overall figure for those with a drug problem was 28 per cent, for those appearing on burglary charges it was 48 per cent—and that in both instances the figure had doubled during the period of the study.

All probation officers need a good basic understanding of the relationship between the individual's substance abuse and their offending. The links may be complex and there may be many layers of excuses to peel away, but effective work will be possible if the supervising officer can:

- develop and encourage the motivation of the individual to change

• collaborate with the specialist agencies who provide skilled help and treatment.

Motivational interviewing is a specific technique that is widely used in this area. It identifies six clear stages that cover the entire course of change, including any relapse, and forms a useful framework for both the probation officer and offender to understand the process. (The model, which was developed by two psychologists, is described in Prochaska and DiClemente, 1984). It complements a range of awareness and education programmes, on both drink and drugs, in which groupwork reinforces the sessions with the individual. A typical alcohol awareness programme, using slides, videos, written exercises and questionnaires, as well as group discussion, might cover:

• the physical effects of drink
• the link between drink and crime
• the effects on victims of crime
• changing offending behaviour
• strategies for more general change
• planning for an offence-free future.

There are specialist courses for drink drivers which have been particularly successful in demonstrating the effectiveness of this approach. A three year pilot project by the Department of Transport, starting in 1994, made drink-driver rehabilitation programmes available to around 20 courts and probation services were among the providers of these courses, which ran on a national model. A large scale research programme, which compared those who attended the courses with others from 'control' courts elsewhere concluded in its initial report that those who completed the course successfully were three times less likely to reoffend. Research continues and the pilot project (and the number of probation schemes) has expanded considerably, with the hope that it can be extended nationally from the year 2000.

Drug offenders have demanded a wider range of responses, not least because the nature of their addiction means they become prolific and high-risk offenders. A variety of approaches have been tried, from residential treatment facilities to day care and 'drop-in' centres. The new 'drug testing and treatment orders' in the Crime and Disorder Act 1998 should start in 1999 and will add a new and powerful option for courts in dealing with a difficult problem.

One of the most interesting schemes, based on a approach, pioneered in The Netherlands, started in Kent in 1995 and has since been adapted for use in a number of areas. Called the Intensive

Supervision and Support Programme (ISSP) it is a partnership between the police, probation service and health service, which focuses on a small group of ten prolific drug offenders in a particular town. Supervision is provided by all three agencies—the offender attends a drugs clinic, is seen at least three times each week by the probation officer or police officer attached to the scheme and may also be visited at home by staff from either service. The offender also knows that information is shared freely between the services and that increased surveillance is also part of the package. (A picture of the 'top ten' offenders on this scheme could be found in Folkestone police station, where the scheme was piloted—a simple but effective way of ensuring that attention was targeted on those taking part). At the same time, extra help was also available—good access to drug services, the employment advice team from the probation service and anything else needed to get away from the cycle of drugs and crime in which the offenders were trapped. The first ten offenders in Folkestone had over 500 recorded offences between them—a stark reminder of the need to provide effective programmes and the risk if they fail. After 18 months, however, the results were sufficiently impressive to expand the scheme to other areas of Kent and the joint health, police and probation input was expanded accordingly.

WHAT WORKS?

The ISSP was untypical in being carefully researched from the very beginning—a product, no doubt, of the fact that each agency wanted to determine if their investment was justified. More often, new developments have come about as a result of perceived need, individual enthusiasms or local initiatives; most started in faith, rather than from a foundation of previous research results. The results, inevitably, were mixed and while there were some very creative and successful programmes, other probation areas were frequently unaware of what had been achieved, and made the same mistakes and discoveries in reinventing the process all over again.

During the 1990s, however, increasing attention has been focused, at an international level, on the ways in which offenders might consistently be supervised more effectively in the community. Much of the evidence comes from research into very structured and defined groupwork programmes and it covers both the methods which are most likely to be successful and the offenders with whom such programmes should be used. In Britain, the work has been strongly promoted by the Probation Inspectorate and has culminated in a report *Strategies for*

Effective Offender Supervision (see *Further Reading*) and an *Effective Practice Guide,* which will be increasingly influential in practice development over the next few years.

The 'What Works' approach does not invent anything startlingly new. What it does do is impose a rigorous and consistent structure on an area of work for which previous claims and counter-claims had been made on, often slender, evidence. It looks at six main areas:

- *targeting and assessment* in which matching learning styles and abilities, clear eligibility criteria and effective assessment and selection are emphasised
- *programme design* based on clear models of change and research evidence, linked to appropriate techniques
- *programme delivery* emphasising absolute consistency and positive behaviour modelling
- *case management* to ensure work is integrated within the total probation order
- *proper evaluation and monitoring*
- *good staffing,* in terms of skill, knowledge and ownership of, and commitment to the programme.

'What Works' principles are not simply appropriate to discrete programmes. They can inform individual work, community service and much of the varied work which probation officers manage or deliver. They offer the chance to demonstrate effectiveness in ways which satisfy the increased demand for accountability which all public services must now meet. And they could be influential in increasing public belief and confidence in community sanctions—perhaps the most important gain of all.

Help with employment
Defining what works is only one part of the equation. Being able to identify the factors which make failure more likely is equally important in terms of assessing risk and planning work within the probation order. A large scale reconviction survey (Oldfield: see *Further Reading*) produced compelling evidence of the factors most associated with further offending. Some, including drug abuse, have already been noted; others, linked to offending within the family, or social problems reinforce individual studies elsewhere. High in the list was unemployment, which doubled the odds of reoffending. While not a surprise—employment brings with it a legitimate income, status and a working week—it focused attention on the practical strategies which

every probation service could take to try and improve the employability of the people it supervised.

Many areas now have specialist employment advice teams, whose members work closely with probation officers as part of the supervision plan for individual offenders. Others work in partnership with agencies who specialise in this field and involvement in the 'New Deal' arrangements for the longer term unemployed now feature strongly. Getting a job may, in the short term, be unrealistic; basic skills and qualifications or remedial education may be needed as stepping stones, first. Employment officers know that there is a complex mix of issues to be resolved before someone who has been unemployed for some time can return successfully to work. Confidence building prior to making job applications or attending interviews; developing reliability through consistent attendance at a class or activity; identifying areas of interest or experience are all important.

Employment officers link, equally, with Job Centre staff and with individual employers. They do not ask for special treatment for offenders, but a 'level playing field'. Honesty about previous convictions and the offer of careful selection and ongoing support are all influential in achieving this.

CONCLUSION

Probation looks very different now from 30 or 50 years ago, in terms of language, legislation or practice. At one time, the individual probation officer did just about everything for his or her caseload—one to one counselling, running groups, negotiating with employers, social security officials or providers of accommodation, linking with mental health services or whatever was needed. Now, the probation officer has access to a range of specialists; will manage an equal range of resources but retain overall responsibility for his or her cases. Even breach proceedings, in which the offender is returned to court for failing to comply with the conditions of an order, may be undertaken by a specialist colleague.

Yet, underneath . . . the purpose of the order and the ways of achieving change, as well as the needs and problems of those on supervision have stayed remarkably the same. Poverty, social exclusion, a delinquent family or background and a sense of frustration, hopelessness or anger are as evident in any probation caseload now as they were when I first experienced them over 30 years ago. The following cases span that whole period, but who could be sure in which decade they occurred?

CASE STUDIES

Keith

At 23, Keith had finally exhausted the patience of all around him. Brought up in comfortable surroundings, he began to rebel against expectations of him which he feared he could not meet. Behaviour problems at home were paralleled at school, where he was expelled well before his 'A' level course had been completed. He began to experiment with drugs and there were some bizarre and frightening episodes for both his parents and his two younger sisters.

It was concern for the girls which led Keith's parents to insist that he leave home when he was 19, though they have bailed him out—sometimes literally, often financially—many times since. Keith has been on probation twice. Both orders were unsuccessful; the first ended with a prison sentence for a further offence, the second in breach proceedings when he refused to keep to the conditions agreed with his probation officer. A further spell in prison followed. On release he unexpectedly agreed to continue contact with his probation officer. Sometimes he would call in several times during the week, then disappear for ten days or more without warning. But over a six month period he clearly wanted to change and there were real gains—first, to more stable accommodation than the squats he had become used to; then to a specialist drugs clinic and finally, to a job interview. Work in a biscuit factory may not be what his parents had in mind, but they were pleased with progress and a cautious meeting in the probation office was followed by a visit home. It was another three months before probation contact was completed. 'It was work we wanted to do while he was on probation' his supervising officer said. 'We just had to wait until he was ready for it'.

Jason

Jason was 19 when his probation order was made. A disrupted childhood saw both his father and—later—his stepfather serve prison sentences and frequent family moves meant his schooling was both sparse and unsatisfactory. Opting out of education at 14 by continually truanting, he 'lived on his wits'. This meant casual or seasonal work or petty theft and Jason, who had left home at 17 when his stepfather was released from prison, had been in court three times before his first remand in custody.

The probation officer who met him then described him as 'bitter, hopeless and helpless'. She discovered how badly he had wanted to avoid the cycle of petty crime in which he had grown up—and how little he knew of how to do it. Barely able to read or write, he had never had the confidence to attend a proper job interview, sign on for benefit or undertake many of the tasks we take for granted. Other prisoners cynically encouraged him to 'go for the big one' since there was no future in petty theft and, for Jason, most of whose belongings had been stolen from his primitive lodgings as soon as he was arrested, it must have seemed the only way out.

Moira, the probation officer, saw his needs as overwhelming. 'He needed a hostel to teach him basic cooking and hygiene, for a start', she said.

> He was simply not ready for a bedsit and he needed basic literacy help before he could really hold down a job. It would have been easy to write him off as a scruffy, truculent walk-in thief, because that's how he was, on the surface. There just seemed a chance to have a real go at improving things before he became totally unreachable.

Magistrates made the two-year probation order with a condition to live at a probation hostel for up to 12 months. Basic survival skills were the priority but it was his inability to relate to other residents which surfaced as the main problem and twice he 'went missing' for short periods after a fight. Staff described him as the hostel's volcano—always on the point of erupting.

The breakthrough came via the hostel cook. Jason learned the basics from her, then became her constant helper. She repaid him by helping him read, returning to the hostel in the evenings until he had made progress and his confidence improved. Moira then followed this up with more formal help and, when the time came for him to leave the hostel, found a bed-sit nearby so he could still have a lifeline to the hostel, if needed. Help with budgeting, leisure activities, personal possessions and employment all followed before Jason, now almost 22, completed his order. Moira saw him occasionally for almost another two years—visits to introduce a girl friend or talk about a new job or ask advice about a move to a flat—before she felt that Jason really had completed the transition.

Ernie

Ernie, a 50-year-old, was made subject to a probation order for an apparent first offence of sexual abuse. Intensive work was needed by both his probation officer and a local psychiatrist when it became clear that a long and extensive pattern of offences against children had occurred—and that they were interspersed with alcoholic episodes into which he retreated in self-disgust. Working through that disgust, through denial and self pity was a painstaking process and despite additional help provided by Alcoholics Anonymous and his local

65

Church (to whom he courageously admitted his difficulties) the order ended with the probation officer far from confident. The last few months were spent in devising relapse prevention strategies through his own network of family, friends, employer and church, in an attempt to ensure that progress could be maintained.

●　●　●

Probation remains as varied, as complex, as difficult and occasionally as rewarding as the people who agree to be supervised. Understanding them and helping them understand themselves goes on regardless of legislation, social work trends and fashions and apparent changes in our wider society. This can only remain true while politicians and others still wish the sentence to operate broadly, as it does now. If that overall context changes radically—and there are some aspects of changes in youth justice which suggest that it could—then some difficult choices will have to be made. Alternative models, especially those in which the Probation Service is closely aligned with the overall process of prosecution and is seen as a community punishment agency are readily apparent; the task is to demonstrate the effectiveness of the model which has evolved, and which this book describes.

CHAPTER 5

Hostels

The use of approved probation hostels under a condition of residence in a probation order has a long history. It was recognised early in the nineteenth century that homelessness was a major factor in reoffending and the first societies to help discharged prisoners, which date from the 1820s, were frequently preoccupied with finding men and women suitable places to live. So were the early police court missionaries (*Chapter 1*), who often included plans for settled accommodation in the proposals they put to courts. The term 'hostel', however, is a convenient shorthand for a wide variety of provision and regimes and it is necessary to separate out some of the very different strands of development before concentrating on the group which concerns us most—approved probation hostels.

The statutory hostel sector is only a small part of overall provision. The independent and voluntary sectors, some of which have close links with the probation service, are an essential provider—but would justify a separate book of their own. They have been enormously influential in the development of approved hostels and they still provide a range of specialist services—for drug and alcohol abusers, for the mentally disordered, for sex offenders, for instance—which the statutory sector cannot. Probation service involvement, which grew from many local and charitable bodies had two main strands.

BACKGROUND DATA

The first of these had its origins in the 1920s, when approved probation hostels were first designated. At first they dealt with people aged under 21 only; this remained the case even after the Criminal Justice Act 1948, which introduced a scheme of statutory approval, linked with the provision of public funds.

It was 1969 when experiments with adults began; by 1971 there were over 30 approved hostels—17 for young men under 21, seven for young women and six which could offer places to men aged up to 30. The total number of bed spaces then was 565, but plans to expand it rapidly to 1,650 adult places were already under way.

In parallel, 'after-care' hostels, financed by the Home Office but run by voluntary bodies, were also expanding. The scheme had only started in 1965 (though building on the long history of help to discharged

67

prisoners) and growth—from 55 hostels in 1968 to 116 in 1971—had been very satisfactory. Probation hostels offered very structured and supportive regimes, often with a higher staff ratio, but after-care hostels covered a broader spectrum, including offering a 'half-way house' or an equivalent of a bed-sitting room scheme as a way back to independent living.

Hostels remained a significant—though often under-used and under-valued—option throughout the 1980s but seemed peripheral to the main business of supervision in the community. Some approved hostels developed into a multi-purpose resource, offering bail places for those awaiting trial, the traditional programme for those staying as a condition of a probation order and a facility for offenders on licence or parole. In 1994 a number were closed by the Home Office on a variety of grounds—poor occupancy, cost per place or potential building and maintenance costs—and there are now 100 hostels, mostly very well used indeed.

THE MODERN-DAY HOSTEL

Most hostels have a senior probation officer/manager and a probation officer/deputy manager. Many assistant managers, who provide continuous cover on a shift basis and act as 'key workers' to individual residents are working towards a qualification in probation or social work and using the practical experience gained in the hostel as a preparation for later training, as well as a job in its own right. It is a difficult, but rewarding way in and the direct experience of working with anxious and volatile offenders in the intense and crowded conditions of a hostel offers a stern test.

Purpose
The purpose of approved hostels, as defined in the 1995 National Standards is 'to provide an enhanced level of supervision to enable certain bailees and offenders to remain under supervision in the community'. Hostels can specify their own admissions policy (some still concentrate on bail cases, for instance) but they are *not* expected to be used where homelessness is the only problem. There are other, less expensive options, for that. National Standards, instead, simply define who should *not* be accepted as a prospective resident:

- those whose offences are too minor to justify a hostel placement
- those whose admission would pose an unacceptable risk of harm to staff, other residents or the immediate community

- those who might be at risk from other residents; and as mentioned earlier
- people who are simply homeless. (Some exceptions to this last rule are possible for temporary placements where custody is the only other option).

In practice, a good deal of skill in assessing and managing risk is required when decisions on accepting residents are made, and hostel staff use both discretion and judgement before choices are confirmed. Is an arsonist or someone with very violent offences to be automatically excluded? What are the risks of either a single drug or alcohol abuser and are they increased if there are several residents at the same time? Is the hostel going through a welcome period of stability or a volatile and difficult time? All these, as well as available bed spaces, come into decisions on referrals.

Hostel residents are expected to go to work, if possible, or to attend projects, training courses or treatment facilities in the community. The supportive and structured environment is there to enhance supervision and improve the chances of staying free of crime and this is achieved by:

- creating and sustaining a constructive relationship between hostel staff and residents. The 'modelling' which staff provide is a key to this
- helping develop social and education skills with a view to finding employment; and
- developing leisure interests and the constructive use of time, especially by accessing local community facilities.

HOSTELS IN PRACTICE

On arrival at the hostel, a new resident will go through a planned induction process which covers familiarity with hostel rules and routines; drug, alcohol and health issues; housing benefit and other practical money matters (so that rent payments are covered) confidentiality rules and details of house meetings . . . all the bewildering components of any new institution, however small.

Most hostels operate a *key worker* system in which each staff member takes particular responsibility for a small number of offenders and, within the shift pattern, takes the lead on:

69

- developing an individual plan to make the best use of their stay—the equivalent of a supervision plan in the probation order and, equally, with offence-related problems as the main focus
- examining how community-based resources can be accessed to develop a more constructive lifestyle
- trying to ensure the individual becomes a constructive member of the hostel community itself; and in due course
- planning for eventual departure from the hostel with appropriate 'move-on' plans.

No-one should underestimate the difficulties of working in a hostel setting, where probation staff of all grades meet the reality of the disturbed and difficult behaviour of many offenders at first hand—and often in a particularly intense way. Communal living has its own pressures, quite apart from the individual problems that residents bring; the episodic nature of shift working means that the staff team has to work very closely together, and trust each other's judgement. Yet the gains can be correspondingly large. Rapid change in the 'pressure cooker' of a hostel environment is not only possible—it is often very visible and hostels regularly achieve improbable success stories against considerable odds.

Hostel rules—and the penalties for not complying with them—have to be clear and explicit. Hostels will have a night curfew, but considerable freedom is otherwise enjoyed and the easy availability of drugs and alcohol outside the hostel provide hazards that staff have to face on a regular basis. Rules include prohibitions on:

- violent, threatening or disruptive language or conduct
- threatening or abusive behaviour as a result of drink or drugs
- theft or damage; and
- conduct that might give offence to staff, residents or members of the public

and appropriate action has to be equally clear. Formal warnings may be given by hostel staff but more serious breaches return to court. For an offender on bail, the withdrawal of the bail place will normally mean a return to custody; for those on probation the court will need to decide whether the order can continue and, if not, how the court should re-sentence. In either case, hostel staff must be prepared to prove the breach in court and to express a view on whether or not a return to the hostel is recommended.

Many of the offenders who need hostel placements come from disturbed and fractured backgrounds, with little experience of 'normal' life. Loving relationships have been rare; physical and sexual abuse; and uncaring and indifferent parenting are evident all too often. Many have been in children's' homes or other institutions and regard yet another placement with hostility. Most, when asked, want an independent flat or bed-sit, even though they may not be ready or able to cope with independent living.

Within this framework, hostel staff—from the cook to the manager—have to build up trust, confidence, social and living skills. They have to act as adult role models, coax, cajole and control in equal measure and try—in the six months that is usually available—to move offenders on to other accommodation with less likelihood of reoffending. At the same time, good relationships have to be maintained with the local community.

Hostels have to provide a consistent, stable environment when—in reality—almost all go through recurring crises which reflect the volatile group they contain. It is probably the toughest task in the probation service.

CHAPTER 6

Community Service

In 1973 a tentative start was made in six probation areas on a new sentence of the court. The community service order, under which an offender agrees to work unpaid for between 40 and 240 hours, is perhaps—with the fine—the simplest and clearest of all penalties imposed on offenders.[1] Offences impose a cost on the community; offenders are given a chance to make some reparation and overcome some of the harm caused by the crime. Depriving offenders of their leisure time is a punishment but, it was hoped, constructive activity might also lead to a changed outlook.

Twenty five years later, community service orders as pioneered in England and Wales have spread, worldwide, to more than 40 countries. The sentence is probably the most successful penal innovation since the Second World War. In 1996, 63,400 new community service orders started, 17,100 of them as an integral part of a combination order. Six million hours of free labour were provided for over 17,000 individuals and groups and countless community facilities were improved—a monument to the positive contribution that offenders can also make.

For Probation Services, the organization of community service by offenders has become a core task; indeed, some would see it, now, as the 'flagship' order. Between 1992 and 1995, the numbers of new orders exceeded the number of probation orders and although is no longer the case the numbers are still very close. The range of project work undertaken is vast—from landscaping play areas to decorating village halls; working with the disabled and elderly; cleaning up graffiti and beaches; large scale environmental work and maintaining footpaths—anything which serves a useful purpose and enables offenders to pay something back to the community.

Yet the idea is not completely new. It can be traced back to medieval times, when offenders convicted of petty offences such as drunkenness, brawling and theft could be ordered to perform a number of 'day wens' in addition to the 200 or so which were already due to the Lord of the Manor in return for accommodation and the strip of land which provided basic subsistence. A period of enlistment at sea, or in the armed forces, in place of any other penalty was also common and could be considered a forerunner to community service. Certainly, for 200 years it formed a useful way of keeping recruitment numbers up, and prison numbers down.

THE ORIGINS OF COMMUNITY SERVICE

In 1970 the Advisory Council on the Penal System noted a widespread recognition among sentencers that a new non-custodial penalty was required and suggested that offenders should be required to engage in unpaid service to the community. The Wootton Rèport ('Non Custodial and Semi-Custodial Penalties'), which developed the idea, was both idealistic and clear headed. The intention was that the sentence would be punitive, for the offender would be deprived of his or her leisure time. Yet they were determined to avoid the 'chain gang' approach and to resist schemes with an element of humiliation or punishment for its own sake. An offender was not to undergo 'some form of penance related directly to his offence . . . but to perform service of value to the community or to those in need'.

Indeed, it was hoped that constructive activity in the community might also result in a changed outlook on the part of the offender. Baroness Wootton's committee thought there were numerous voluntary organizations which would welcome offenders to work with them and that shared enterprise would lead to shared values. This idealism can be seen in the best projects, but all too often offender groups work *for* other organizations rather than *with* them, since the number of offenders often far outstrips the number of volunteers. But different kinds of gains—the discipline of a work habit, practical skills, a sense of belonging, as well of achievement—are all possible, too, within a well-run community service order and the high hopes of the Committee and Parliament have been more than fulfilled.

Community service started on 1 January 1973, its introduction having been made possible by the Criminal Justice Act 1972. In the early discussions it was by no means clear who would be asked to run it, but after considering several alternatives the Probation Service was chosen. It already had a national network, was involved in work with offenders and operated in and with the courts. Not for the first time, developments were being hastened by a rising prison population and considerable unrest within prisons, and no time was lost in starting a pilot project involving five probation areas—Nottinghamshire, Durham, Kent, Inner London and South West Lancashire.

Fears were expressed that the work undertaken would eat into a shrinking job marked for paid workers, but the Trades Union Congress had resolved to work to reduce the prison population and was prepared to support community service. Local Committees often had a trades union representative in the early days and the practical help they provided was enormously useful. Other fears, from within the Probation Service, were that the necessarily strong elements of control and imposed discipline would change the nature and values of the service. They probably have, and for the better, although tensions between the two areas of work are still visible, especially in the supervision of combination orders (i.e. when probation and community service are combined in a single sentence: see below).

The Home Office Research Unit monitored the pilot projects and around 1,200 orders were made in the first 18 months. The scheme was pronounced viable and although, then, there had been no noticeable effect on the prison population there was enough enthusiasm for the scheme to be made available nationally in April 1975.

Early experience
Community service was, from the very beginning, an option which, (with its elements of punishment, retribution and rehabilitation) offered something to almost everyone. All these were overlaid with the possibility of it serving as an alternative to custody but its position in the 'tariff' of community penalties has always been ambiguous. Punishment through work, or keeping idle hands busy, was always likely to be appealing; yet the rehabilitative element of self-improvement through the completion of worthwhile tasks was clearly there to be exploited, too.

Above all, community service offers an approach which does not start from the standpoint of problems, or negative and difficult issues. Instead, the starting point can be: 'What do you think you can offer?' Set alongside this the aims for the scheme as defined in the Nottinghamshire pilot project and there is a powerful option for change. These four aims were that community service should:

- be a worthwhile experience for the offender
- offer tangible benefits to the community
- generally take place in or near a person's locality
- offer offenders a chance to continue service after the order expired.

Initially, there were attempts to make community service a direct alternative to imprisonment, rather than a more wide ranging penalty. The Wootton Committee saw it as potentially both, and the legislation certainly allowed this by being non-prescriptive as to its use. Both the Court of Appeal and the Home Office seemed to favour the 'last resort before custody' approach, but with courts left able to use it as they saw fit wide variations in use were inevitable. The controversy was not finally resolved until the Criminal Justice Act 1991 replaced the concept of alternatives to prison with proportionality, or 'just deserts'.

74

Right from the start it was clear that imaginative, well-run projects were likely to get a positive response from offenders, while dull repetitive tasks might gain sullen acceptance—and sometimes not even that. An early project required offenders to clear paper and other debris from a boundary fence at a rubbish tip by the side of a main railway line. The work was futile since, in the absence of good management of the tip, more debris accumulated as quickly as it was cleared. It caused some amusement to passengers, but offenders soon refused to work on the project.

Yet another project, to clear rubbish from a beach, has been in operation for many years and gets cheerful co-operation from its workers. The local council—which benefits from the coveted 'Blue Flag' award the beach received—makes its gratitude clear; local residents, who value the regular weekend working parties, often bring refreshments to 'their' workers, and supervisors manage to maintain a sense of fun as well as hard work by introducing elements of competition and even the occasional driftwood barbecue into what is—still—an unending task. Community service organizers and supervisors learnt quickly what Gill McIvor from the University of Stirling later documented through careful research—that work perceived as worthwhile and positive produces better attendance, more satisfactory completion rates, and less subsequent reoffending. Community service is still seen as punishment by those on the receiving end, in terms of both the imposition of work and the deprivation of liberty—but it works.

TYPES OF PLACEMENT

The framework for community service is firmly set by National Standards, which define the main purpose of the order as being to prevent further offending by re-integrating the offender into the community through:

- punishment—by means of positive and demanding unpaid work, keeping to disciplined requirements; and
- reparation to the community—by undertaking socially useful work.

Once the order is made by the court, the offender has to be assessed; principally in terms of risk, but also taking into account his or her skills or preferences, and any indications the court may have given about the type of work it envisaged.

In issuing National Standards, the Home Office listed the criteria which placements should meet. They should:

75

- be demanding, in the sense of being physically, emotionally or intellectually taxing (and requiring 'significant effort')
- demonstrate benefit to the community through crime prevention, environmental improvements, help and care for the elderly, handicapped or disabled; or improved amenities or appearance of a neighbourhood
- encourage a sense of personal responsibility and self discipline
- meet health and safety requirements
- undertake work which would *not* otherwise be done by paid employees
- be assessed to ensure that the location and nature of *any* community service activity could not give the impression of providing a reward for offending. Placements should never take place abroad.

This last requirement needs some further explanation, later, but the list, which was drawn up at a time when ministers were obsessed with 'toughening up' community penalties, was much more to do with their view of enhancing public confidence than of running an effective community service scheme. The two are not incompatible, but most community service schemes need a basic mix of the following:

- *large scale environmental projects*: these provide regular work over long periods and can cope with fluctuating numbers. Offenders often work alongside other volunteer conservation groups in canal restoration, river and footpath maintenance, work with the National Trust, woodland clearance or providing disabled access to beaches.

- *painting and decorating groups:* there seems to be an inexhaustible supply of work in this area—village halls and other community facilities, schools (often in conjunction with PTA work groups), individual homes (for the elderly or disadvantaged) and one-off projects which have ranged from the Cutty Sark to Radio Caroline.

- *groups to meet specific local needs:* organisers are asked to respond to a huge variety of requests, now that community service schemes are so well established. Lunch clubs for the elderly, furniture for playgroups, restoration of an overgrown churchyard, converting unused shops into a community centre for a Bangladeshi community, gardening for the elderly and housebound. The list is endless.

- *individual or agency placements:* these use supervisors from the receiving agency—a hospital, old people's home, charity shop or school, for instance—rather than a work group with a supervisor paid by the Probation Service. Offenders need to be carefully selected, and good liaison with the nominated agency supervisor is needed, but placements with just one or two offenders in this way can be very successful indeed. Offenders develop a real sense of belonging and of being valued. Many grow in confidence and some do, indeed, continue as ordinary volunteers when the court order expires.

In case this seems impossibly optimistic, it is as well to recognise the day-to-day difficulties with which community service staff have to cope. For the offenders are, all too often, poorly motivated, unused to any sort of work habit, affected by drink or drugs or both, unskilled and unself-confident and with few of the very basic social or other skills that working in a group, or with other people, demands. Yet work must start within ten working days of the order being made, a minimum work rate of five hours per week must be maintained and disciplined timekeeping, including travel to work sites will be needed. Failure to turn up, or comply properly with the order must be swiftly followed up and only two formal warnings are allowed before a return to court.

Community service staff have to be realistic about what can be achieved—encouraging, cajoling, threatening until offenders settle into a work routine which may be little more than manageable—but which may turn out to be enjoyable. Some areas run workshops for those offenders who are too risky or too vulnerable to be allowed, even with supervision, to join more open groups in the community. At the other end of the scale, national celebrities such as Eric Cantona, the footballer or Chris Eubank, the boxer, need to be accommodated in work which uses their talents for the benefit of others, but still meets the needs of the sentence. There was a good deal of public debate about Eric Cantona's order—whose natural talents as someone who was already an idol was put to a demanding teaching programme for hundreds of schoolchildren in the Manchester area who would not otherwise have had this chance. However, indicative of the adaptability of community service to differently assessed needs, another international footballer, Vinny Jones, the former Wimbledon player, was accommodated within a group of offenders undertaking property renovation.

Community service is, in fact, a very flexible sentence, both in terms of hours—the range of 40-240 hours allows for wide variation of use from relatively minor offences to those which might otherwise have resulted in a prison sentence—and in terms of what it can achieve.

Around 75 to 80 per cent of orders are successfully completed, though a significant proportion of offenders are warned, or taken back to court before this is finally achieved. It is true that many of these, too, are completed without enthusiasm, a grudging acceptance of the requirements of the order the only reason for compliance.

Equally, for many young offenders in particular, the order may be a revelation in terms of what they can offer to other people; what they can achieve, or the skills they can acquire. Two very different projects in Kent demonstrate this particularly well.

Two working examples
The first, starting out as a very practical group, eventually had much more to offer.

A renovation project
A cerebral palsy charity, whose day care facilities were already fully stretched, was offered an unused, almost derelict school in which to expand, but had no funds for the extensive conversion work which would be needed. Two community service officers, Tim Reeves and Janice Youseman describe what followed:

> The school was in an extremely sorry state of repair, comprehensively vandalised, all doors, windows and skylights boarded up and thus absolutely pitch black inside, the gloom only enlivened by the sound of feet scrunching across shards of broken glass. A daunting prospect? Well nigh impossible, we thought. But Eric Earnshaw, from the charity, was a man with a vision. He wanted the best, the very best, for his guests; the huge hall's plain painted brick walls would not do. They must be plastered. New administrative offices, workrooms, toilets, bathrooms, shower rooms suitable for wheelchair users, activity rooms . . . and this in a building which had been designed for small children, with everything appropriately tiny. None of the existing fixtures would do!

The original idea was for community service offenders to decorate the building, once the huge amount of building work had been completed. But, as it happened, the community service officers were visionaries, too. Despite never having undertaken work on this scale before, they knew that their own 'workforce' responded well to interesting and varied work, especially if children or disabled adults were the beneficiaries.

> We therefore offered to take on both building and decoration, secure in the knowledge that one of our supervisors, Brian Forster, had already achieved good results on smaller building projects. We are, of course, dependent on who the courts send us, and that is on the basis of offences committed and

not on the skills required! But fate took a hand — as if by magic we were sent a bricklayer with a long order and later a plasterer, carpenter and fully qualified electrician. In all our years of service we had never known such bounty!

Actual work started in January. It took eight workers two full days to clear up broken glass and other debris and to isolate and repair damaged wiring. No less than 74 skips were eventually filled. In the early days every window, door and skylight was boarded up and these make-shift shutters had to be removed at the start of every work-day and replaced at the end — a tiresome but very necessary precaution against vandalism.

Thirteen new rooms were constructed, plastered, wired and decorated; shower rooms and toilets plumbed and tiled; flat roofs repaired and garden wheelchair paths laid. Anyone who thinks community service is a soft option should have seen the pace of work in freezing cold conditions . . . and in temperatures in the 90s in a boiling hot summer.

All our workers learned fresh skills and improved existing ones. Some were able to gain paid employment as a direct result of what they had learned; Tony, a trainee bricklayer who had despaired of ever reaching "commercial" speeds, who gained both the speed and confidence required on a building site and Justin, who was a concrete renderer who longed to be a plasterer and who not only gained employment in his chosen trade but also returned as an unpaid volunteer to help complete the project.

The commitment displayed by Justin and others well after their court order had been discharged, was a special feature of the project. As the charity began to use the half-completed building, so offenders began to see children, in particular, who were more disadvantaged than they would ever be. The response was instinctive and encouraging. Over 100 workers completed well over 4,000 hours at the centre and, as it moved towards full usage, it was particularly rewarding to see how the potential to use carefully selected offenders in care work, as well as in building and maintenance, was being recognised.

Working with the disadvantaged

The second project within the same geographical area, required very different skills. Carefully selected offenders, with their supervisors, organized a series of 'Discovery Clubs' for young adults with learning difficulties or other handicaps. For a full day, the offenders took care of someone much more disadvantaged than themselves, and provided all the help and attention needed—feeding, washing, toileting as well as joining in games or other simple activities. It is sometimes physically exhausting; often emotionally demanding, but there are three distinct beneficiaries:

- the young adults who enjoy a full day of attention, company and stimulation
- their parents, who have a priceless day's respite from the remorseless demands of care; and
- the offenders themselves since—as with the Cerebral Palsy Unit—their perspective on life, their own situation and their sense of work are inevitably altered.

Other types of schemes

Other schemes produce different benefits. One routine churchyard maintenance job became a full scale archaeological dig when workers discovered a second level of building several feet below the known footings. The project was extended to uncover the new foundations and the detective work involved in gradually revealing a Saxon site kept workers enthused for months. At another rural chuchyard, the congregation were so impressed with the achievement of a small group of offenders that they frankly spoiled them; afternoon tea became more of a picnic and quite apart from the ginger cake, the sense of being valued by a group whose only other image was of being tearaways is what will stay for longest. At the Battle of Britain Memorial site, a windswept down near Dover, World War II veterans talked easily and with natural respect to tattooed young men who maintained the site—a physically demanding task. On learning that they were offenders on community service orders, the reaction was usually a wry comment to the effect that the veterans too, were wild once—but there were different opportunities to show it.

Vocational qualifications

In the last two years, real progress has been made in combining the work and discipline of community service with a basic vocational qualification—something many young offenders never achieved at school. Both the structure of the order and the opportunities it brings makes the potential enormous and the Vocational Access Certificate, a very basic but useful introduction to a range of skills, knowledge of health and safety procedures and good work practices, is now achieved by increasing numbers of offenders on community service orders.

For all the obvious positives, completion of community service hours is not an easy process, especially where the interest and enthusiasm of the offender is not engaged. Thirty per cent of orders go back to court at some stage for a breach of the order's requirements and many more require formal warnings from Probation Service staff to encourage them through. Those who return to court are often fined and given a second chance to complete their hours—and take it.

Success on community service—in terms of a basic qualification, a newly acquired skill, a real sense of achievement or acceptance—is a bonus. The order does not set out to deal with offending behaviour and all too often staff realise that 'their' worker is likely to return to a lifestyle unchanged by the experience. The requirement is a simple 'paying-back'; a sense of having wiped the slate clean for that particular offence. By this standard, the high percentage who complete their hours as specified *are* a success—but a 48 per cent reoffending rate (Kent Reconviction Survey) in two years demonstrates just how cautious services need to be in making claims for long-term, large scale effects. But a sentence which combines cheapness (£33 per offender per week at 1996 figures) with substantial benefit to the community, deserves to be judged on a number of criteria and in terms of the 'added value' it provides community service deserves the description it received (in a newspaper not known for sympathetic coverage) as 'the most successful penal innovation since the Second World War.'

FUTURE POTENTIAL

Until the implementation of the Criminal Justice Act of 1991, a probation order and a community service order could not be combined as a penalty for a single offence. Now, they can. From 40 to 100 hours of community service can be combined with from a 12 month (as opposed to the standard six month) to three year probation element—and sentencers have relished the opportunity to impose a portion of punishment alongside the help they see as the main benefit of probation, i.e. supervision. The combination order has spread far beyond the limited application—for 'the most serious offences within the community penalty band'—first envisaged to become an established option in its own right, rather as the community service order had done two decades earlier. New orders made have grown as follows:

1992	1,400
1993	9,200
1994	12,600
1995	14,800
1996	17,100
1997	19,000 (Estimated figure after nine months)

Such orders have not been without their problems. Essentially two different orders, supervised by two different people and with two sometimes varying sets of expectations, a good deal of co-operation is needed if the supervision plan is to work well. The disciplined pace required in community service may seem at odds with equally

81

demanding but more individually tailored patterns of work on probation. The probation element requirements (especially if they include additional conditions in respect of special groups or drug and alcohol treatment) may be at the limit of the offenders' capacity and close liaison, support and—sometimes—tolerance are needed if the order is to be consistently and well managed. But the rapid growth of combination orders is very much part of the developing potential of community service.

Another potential growth area is the use of community service orders in cases of fine default, where a set number of hours can be worked to pay off an outstanding fine. At present only available in two experimental project areas, it nevertheless seems popular with sentencers and will grow—if it is allowed to. There are real dangers in overloading community service schemes with offenders for whom it was not, originally, thought an appropriate sentence and some caution should be exercised before unlimited expansion is allowed.

It is still possible to be constructively critical about community service—ensuring equal access for women and ethnic minority groups needs continuing work and so, too, does the development of a proper career structure for staff in the community service sphere. But in just over two decades, community service has moved from becoming an interesting new option to an equal partner as 'market leader' in the overall work of the Probation Service. It has been at the forefront of new developments, such as National Standards; has had a profound impact on how we think about offenders and recognise their capacity for achievement and for good; and is the key to good external relations— the positive, visible face of the Probation Service.

Future development is partly about sustaining a high quality service to both the courts and the community; about producing good results from often unpromising material and filling the gaps in community provision for the elderly and handicapped, about taking on tasks that no-one else can be found to do, about demonstrating that offenders *can* give something back. Why, then, should the Home Office guidance mentioned earlier need that extra clause about community service *never* giving the impression of providing a reward for offending and *never* taking place abroad? The answer lies in one of the most imaginative projects ever undertaken; an area for growth which could still exploit its potential to the full.

A ground breaking initiative
The idea of taking a group of community service offenders abroad grew from a conversation between the chief probation officer of Surrey, Michael Varah, and a journalist (an ex-probation officer) who had just

returned from Romania, in 1990. It developed into a partnership with a local community church and the Surrey Care Trust and by Easter 1991 the first project was under way—an impressive feat in itself, given the enormous logistical and planning problems.

The project had two main aims; to provide a modest amount of humanitarian aid to a country whose needs were urgent and overwhelming; and to provide a unique work programme for offenders that would develop their sense of responsibility and reduce their offending behaviour. They were to work at a large orphanage at Deva, in central Romania. It held 500 children and the report proposing the scheme pulled no punches as it described the task ahead:

> The majority of the children are young but some have remained at the orphanage beyond their teens and are now in their early twenties. A number suffer from mental and/or physical disability. The very young sleep two to a cot, and the older ones four to a bed. The heating system is never adequate and frequently breaks down. Each room is crammed with beds or cots. The mattresses are soiled. The walls have not been painted for many years. There are no decorations or personal effects to be seen. The atmosphere smells of urine. The task for our offenders will be very demanding.

Eventually, the specific project chosen was the total refurbishment of a children's hospital of 110 beds and the organization would have put off all but the most determined. All materials for redecoration, repair, electrical and plumbing systems had to be taken from the UK and so, too, did supplies for the whole party, who had to be completely self-sufficient so as not to be an impossible burden on their impoverished hosts. The local press was hostile, the team was under intense scrutiny from a television team. Yet it had not only to complete its work—it had to encourage local volunteers to sustain the work after its departure. There were moments when it seemed unlikely that it would even start. Fuelled by adverse press comment, the local authorities in Deva were so terrified of the 'ruthless gangsters' who had appeared that, initially, they refused permission for them even to unload their trucks.

Astonishingly, it worked. No-one who saw the resulting television documentary on the trip could fail to be impressed and moved by the reaction of the young community service workers and the response they achieved. Work went on for nine hours each day, far in excess of the actual community service orders, and the sense of working as a team was very apparent as large parts of the dilapidated and depressing hospital were restored to life.

Even more astonishingly, the Surrey Probation Service were later subject to substantial criticism from the Home Office, who complained that the project did not fulfil the requirement that work should benefit *the community offended against* and that various requirements of the scheme, including the maximum number of hours to be worked in any one week, were being infringed. With very considerable support from sentencers, Surrey decided to continue.

The second trip involved 19 offenders, against the 11 who had first taken part. They, too, had to raise money for their own expenses. The second group was carefully chosen, well briefed and had some experience of working together as they all undertook the first 21 hours of their order in a geriatric hospital in Surrey. But two had to be sent home because of disruptive behaviour fuelled by the easy availability of strong, cheap local beer and two others were involved in a fracas the night before the return trip. The pressures of two hard, demanding weeks work were, it seems, matched by pressures which surfaced locally, after dark.

The majority, however, responded as positively as expected and indeed the behaviour of almost all of them has been a tribute to the impact which the experience provided. Three years later, only one had re-offended; almost all agreed it had changed both their attitudes to life, to their values and behaviour; and two have returned voluntarily to Romania to work with a charitable relief agency. The *Daily Mirror* summed it up under the heading 'Now that Really *is* Community Service' and with the by-line 'Mission Impossible'.

The Home Office remained unconvinced, and added the specific requirement that 'placements should never take place abroad' in the 1995 National Standards. Given the supportive media stance indicated above, this seems to be a curiously blinkered view, for other admirable organisations such as Raleigh International are acutely aware of the value of community service projects as part of their overall expedition plans (for offenders and non-offenders alike). Perhaps a more rational re-think will allow this restriction to change. Large-scale community service projects abroad are neither feasible nor desirable, but the Surrey project caught the imagination of staff, sentencers and offenders alike. A few 'landmark' projects of this kind help create and shape wider attitudes—it was noticeable following the first project how the number of orders made in the Surrey courts rose steadily. It was a high risk venture, for these were high risk offenders and a serious incident in Romania could have had undue repercussions. But the gains in personal terms, and the enormous impact on the life of a very deprived community must be worth developing.

THE BENEFICIARIES

Back at home, community service staff regularly survey their beneficiaries—the thousands of organizations and individuals who receive workers, and benefit from the unpaid labour. Charities, local groups and the elderly, as well as national and regional volunteer bodies all appreciate the benefits which accrue; most, too, are realistic enough to know that it will not always be plain sailing.

A recent survey in Kent, of 95 beneficiaries, produced a 100 per cent affirmative answer to the question: 'Would you use community service again, or recommend it to others'? but in the comments on specific questions there was an acknowledgement that such positive views are only achieved through hard work:

All problems were quickly and appropriately dealt with by staff

Some of them worked really hard but others do not want to get out of the van

Team well behaved but clearly not everyone wanted to be involved with the work they were doing

One respondent, while praising the work, added:

We still have fixed views in the village from those who do not want them here

Others had their views changed:

A better understanding and a more open-ended attitude towards offenders, as a result

We now have a very positive view of offenders through our liaison and their work

And, most frankly of all

We have come to realise that they are just people who have committed an offence, not an alien species.

The 'added value' that community service provides through its very practical work is incalculable but it may be that last comment which points to the most important gain. By its visibility as well as its worth; its impact on the lives of thousands of individuals and of communities, this is one sentence which is helping shape views on offenders and on the sentencing process itself. The Probation Service has much to be proud of in the way it has developed; it is also fortunate to be part of it.

ENDNOTE

[1] For a comprehensive account of the history and practice of community service, see *Paying Back: Twenty Years of Community Service,* Whitfield D and Scott D (Eds.), Waterside Press, 1993.

CHAPTER 7

Work in Prisons

The appointment of probation officers to prisons came about as a result of an Advisory Council report, *The Organization of After-Care*, in 1960. The report recommended that probation officers should be seconded to all prisons, as welfare officers, taking over the task from a range of welfare staff (mostly employed by voluntary and charitable organizations) who had previously been in post. The change did not take place until 1966 and the introduction of parole the following year reinforced the very real differences now that the probation service was fully involved.

Previously, the welfare officer was a member of the prison team and accountable to the governor; the new probation officers had a dual responsibility. Still answerable to the governor for day to day work, and still bound by the emphasis on security, discipline and control which every prison imposes, they nevertheless had to keep firmly focused on the world outside. Professionally accountable to their own chief probation officer, they became the link with the outside world in terms of family contacts, release plans, risk assessment and reports to the Parole Board. They provided a social work service to the prison—and a reminder that, all too often, the real work in terms of preventing reoffending would continue long after the gate had shut on discharge day. Four aspects of the probation role in prison were identified early on as:

- a social caseworker
- the focal point of social work
- the normal channel of communication on social problems with the outside world; and
- the planner of after care.

This provided the base on which probation involvement could be built over the next two decades, but progress was often uneven. Probation officers are seconded to prisons; they remain employees of the local Probation Service, but all costs are met by the prison. The isolation of such prison posts from other probation teams, reactions from prison staff that could range from lukewarm to hostile and the feeling that work was swamped by day to day requests for help with visits and other practical issues meant that such postings were often unpopular, resisted and seen in very negative terms.

Such negativism frequently led to a matching response from prison staff, who believed probation officers were: (a) naïve, soft and easily manipulated by prisoners; (b) taking away one of the few positive areas of work they had previously enjoyed; and (c) were 'nine to five' workers who left the prison in all its most difficult periods and had little understanding of how it really functioned.

For two decades, these attitudes were not uncommon. But they were not the only side of the story. Right from the start, talented and far sighted staff from both the Probation Service and the Prison Service realised that there were separate jobs to do, but that a working partnership based on mutual respect and trust could offer a lot of joint satisfaction as well as a better service.

I had the good fortune to work in Coldingley prison in the 1970s. The prison was brand new, with an experimental regime as an industrial prison and trying notions as radical as a free labour market. Staff were refreshingly open to ideas and some inspired leadership meant that these could flourish. In return, the probation team covered the prison from 9 a.m. to 9 p.m. and at weekends, on a shift basis, shared tasks and information with prison officers—including group work—and demonstrated that we, too, had a real commitment to making the prison work.

HM Prison Coldingley was far from alone, and committed staff soon worked on models of good practice in many prisons and in very different settings. In busy local prisons, with a constant turnover of prisoners going to court or serving short sentences, crisis work imposed remorseless demands—issues to sort out before court, immediate fears following arrest, the search for accommodation and employment among them. Training prisons meant an emphasis on trying to use the sentence constructively, planning for release and sustaining all important relationships during the period of separation; and long term prisons, especially those with men serving life sentences, brought different challenges—helping individuality and hope survive, understanding and coming to terms with the most serious offences and being realistic about the future.

Work for probation officers in prisons has always had its enthusiasts—and I am one. One of my colleagues used to describe it as 'the equivalent of a teaching hospital—nowhere else will you find such a collection of acute and interesting cases; nowhere else will you be able to use your skills to better effect'. Even when, as is so often the case, the physical environment is bleak and the demands of security and control seem oppressive there is enormous scope for positive work. For me, the least expected feature was the humour, which is one way that long term prisoners cope with impossible situations; and while some laughter may have been tinged with desperation or hysteria, most was of a gentler kind: a manifestation of an uncrushable human spirit—and an indication that there is plenty for a probation officer to work with, even in this difficult setting.

DEVELOPING THE ROLE

The overlapping responsibilities of prison and probation staff were recognised early and the 1974 'Social Work in Prison' initiative was one of many which emphasised *throughcare*, or resettlement work, as a joint responsibility. This was much more than a concentration on preparations for release—it aimed to relate work in prison (whether on offending behaviour or in acquiring educational or vocational skills) to work which would continue in supervision after release. This process was given even greater emphasis by changes introduced by the Criminal Justice Act 1991.

Now, a prison sentence no longer finishes on release, but is served partly in custody and partly in the community—a process which started with the introduction of parole. Supervision by the probation officer thus becomes part of the punishment, rather than just the offer of help with resettlement for its own sake. It brings the same ambivalent mixture of work that community sentences do, but the discretion which the supervisor can exercise enables a realistic balance to be retained.

The complex mix which makes up the complete sentence will be further confused in January 1999 when Home Detention Curfews are introduced and short periods of electronic monitoring—with or without probation supervision—are also introduced as part of the phased return to freedom (and as a last ditch move to reduce the pressure of numbers on prisons). *Figure 1* sets out the position from that date in simplified form.

National Standards for the supervision of offenders in the community lay down specific responsibilities for seconded officers in prisons; in relation to sentence planning, tackling offending behaviour and establishing continuity of supervision with probation officers working in the community. The 1992 edition stated:

Category	Early Release	Special Conditions	Supervision or Electronic Monitoring	Notes
Young Offenders Institutions	Automatic at halfway point	Supervision may be by Probation or Social Services YOT	3 months or to halfway point of sentence, whichever is longer	Supervision ends earlier if 22nd birthday reached
Adult Offenders Sentence less than 3months	Unconditional at halfway point	None	None	
Sentence of 3months to less than 12months	Automatic at halfway point. On electronic monitoring, between 2-8 weeks earlier subject to risk assessment	Home curfew only. No supervision by Probation Service	14 days minimum 2 months maximum	
Sentence 12 months to less than 4 years	Automatic: at half-way point. On electronic monitoring, 2 months early subject to risk assessment	On licence under supervision subject to recall for breach or reoffending	To three quarters point of original sentence	If further offence in last quarter outstanding term may be added to new sentence
Sentence 4 years or more	Discretionary: from halfway point to the two-thirds point. Automatic: at two thirds point	As imposed by Parole Board	To three quarters point of sentence for both categories	If further offence in last quarter outstanding term may be added to new sentence. Also subject to recall
Mandatory life sentence	No fixed date. Discretionary. Any release on recommendation of Parole Board	Regular progress reports to Home Office	Life	Supervision element of licence may be removed
Discretionary life sentence	After period specified by sentencing court	Regular progress reports to Home Office	Life	Supervision element of licence may be removed
Extended supervision (violent or sexual offenders)			If ordered by judge at point of sentence.	

N.B. All prisoners are 'at risk' until the end of their sentence. If a further imprisonable offence is committed, court may add all or part of the outstanding sentence to any new sentence it imposes.

Prison sentences and Post-release Supervision (from January 1999)
Figure 1

The seconded officer has a key role in ensuring the effective delivery of offender throughcare. This is achieved not only by focusing on the social work task and tackling the offending behaviour of inmates but also by the linking role of the post, bridging the prison and outside probation services . . . central elements of the work of seconded officers are: to contribute to the development by prison staff of the offender's sentence plan; and to contribute to addressing and tackling offending behaviour by helping to meet targets set out in the plan. This process will include helping to identify targets which cannot be met in custody and which can most effectively be handled by the supervising officer during the community part of the sentence'.

Partnership

This was followed by, potentially, the most important blueprint to which a prison probation officer can work—a partnership contract between the prison and probation services launched as the National Framework for Throughcare. This defined the respective roles of the two services and their joint accountability for effective throughcare; set out the key tasks; and covered everything from local agreements to advice on the use of volunteers, local help organisations and agencies.

At the same time, however, budgets for prison probation staff were devolved to individual governors, rather than held by the prison service generally; and financial cuts, combined with a rapidly increasing prison population produced enormous drains at local level. It was a disastrous mixture—what looked like a refreshingly explicit partnership agreement was lost in a crisis-ridden exercise to balance local budgets.

Reduction in numbers

From 1995 to 1997, 25 per cent of prison probation posts were lost—an extraordinary proportion of the seconded workforce. Some work was passed to prison staff or, occasionally, to outside agencies but much was not undertaken at all as the sheer pressure of rising numbers took its toll. Individual prisons held out, recognising that the work undertaken by probation staff was both cost effective and necessary, while some changes, forced by financial pressures, were actually long overdue. But the overall effect was destructive and the partnership hopes expressed in the national Throughcare Framework have all too often been illusory.

Ironically, as this book was being written, prison governors were seeking to recruit *more* probation staff, in order to ensure that risk assessments for the new Home Detention Curfew scheme would be in place. Armed with an additional £4.2m to implement the scheme, they then discovered that the national shortage of probation officers, caused

91

by the abandonment of previous training arrangements, meant that all too often, there were none to be had.

Despite the difficulties, the three main areas—sentence planning, tackling offending behaviour and continuity of supervision—are worth considering in more detail. They provide a realistic picture of the involvement of probation officers, as well as an indication of some of the problems.

SENTENCE PLANNING

The idea of the 'seamless sentence' underpins all the developments in sentence planning—the notion that work before, during and after the period in prison should have a clear and realistic focus on the issues that were crucial to offending behaviour in the first place, and which might be addressed in reducing the risk of reoffending. Were drugs or alcohol, unemployment or relationship difficulties or poor housing and poverty factors in the offence? Are physical or mental health problems a factor? If so, does the offender want to work on them? What programmes might help?

How this works in practice is best described in an extract from the Probation Inspectorate report *The Work of Prison Probation Departments* (1996) (see *List of Further Reading*) which describes sentence planning in operation at Askham Grange Women's Prison.

The sentence planning process begins as soon as a woman arrives at Askham Grange. So far as the probation contribution is concerned, she is interviewed within two days and the reception interview, along with information gathered from the field probation officers, previous prison establishment records, etc. forms the basis of a short written report prepared for the initial sentence planning board which takes place within a week (usually less) of the woman's arrival. It was noted with concern that the probation officer's job is made more difficult by the lack of crucial (pre-sentence report and previous convictions) information being available at the appropriate time.

The probation officers attend the board where preliminary targets are set, i.e. for work, education, offending behaviour programmes, etc. A further sentence planning board 28 days later will add to these preliminary decisions and probation staff will ensure that they have met the inmate again at least once, gathered further information from the field probation officer and begun the information gathering and assessment process in relation to risk factors.

It was clear from observing the sentence planning boards—both initial and review—that the probation officers are the staff who know the inmate best in relation to her domestic and social situation and her past and

92

current offences. Prison staff have a better knowledge of the woman's behaviour in the institution in particular in relation to any rule transgressions. The board process enables these different aspects to be considered (alongside information from education staff), information to be exchanged and plans made jointly with the woman who attends.

Probation staff make a short written contribution to the sentence plan on a *pro forma* devised by the team, the content of which is shared with the inmate and prison staff. The team's quality assurance system relies on the fact that the SPO receives a copy of all sentence plan contributions and, as they often attend sentence planning boards on behalf of each other, they regularly see and check each other's work. The quality of the contributions made by the team and seen during the inspection was generally good.

Ensuring that the best use is made of a prisoner's time in custody will always be a difficult task. Prisoners, already experiencing the pains of imprisonment, may be hostile, subversive or indifferent. Cooperation may be helped by the possibility of early release, but may be more apparent than real. Yet good sentence planning, to which probation staff can make an invaluable contribution, remains a worthwhile aim and a very professional task.

TACKLING OFFENDING BEHAVIOUR

Here, prison probation work is a mirror image of work outside. A range of individual and group approaches can be used, the latter often involving prison staff—wing officers, psychologists, teachers or chaplains—as well as the supervising probation officer. If the sentence plan has correctly defined the overall framework, then work with prisoners can be both purposeful and satisfying, as some of the following examples show.

Brian was 24 and much of his life had been spent in institutions, so an 18 month sentence for burglary was something he felt he could cope with easily. At first, he rejected any help from the probation officer but the prospect of release brought feelings of panic and hopelessness. A hostel place was organized for the first few weeks and a volunteer met him at the prison gate—even the first few hours were a real risk, since his last period of freedom had been only ten days. Recognising when he was ready to accept help—and then working hard on the problems—had been the key to progress.

Graham, aged 26, was serving a long sentence for armed robbery and firearms offences, and had a history of violent crime. Work started on an individual level, encouraging him to use specialist help for medical and psychological problems; helping him to cope with frustration and

93

disappointment instead of exploding in angry and violent outbursts. Help with basic education followed but the probation contact went through a difficult period when it was clear that he was using drugs in prison as a response to boredom and pressure. It was a testing time but the mutual trust built up over months helped to resolve issues and progress was then reinforced by a victim awareness course. The probation officer organized a group which brought offenders like Graham face to face with the victims of their type of offence — including a building society cashier and a petrol station attendant. This contact, reinforced over a period of weeks, had a dramatic effect and, when later released on parole, Graham emerged as a much more mature individual — ready to accept responsibilities, more thoughtful and certainly better able to control his temper.

Malcolm, aged 28, was serving a sentence of five years for robbery. He had brusquely rejected any contact with the prison probation officer during the first part of his sentence and seemed to enjoy the status he acquired in the prison as a 'hard man' and a career criminal. Certainly his long record of offences seemed to indicate that the prospect of change was remote.

Then he learned that Gina, his wife, intended to start divorce proceedings and regarded the marriage as over. She would not visit any more but would allow their two small children to come, with grandparents, nearer the date of his release. Malcolm exploded, lost remission for damaging his cell and seemed, through anger and despair ,to be more volatile than ever.

Contact was established with the home probation officer, who was able to undertake some visits to Gina and the children — not as a basis for reconciliation, but simply to keep some family links alive. Inside the prison, regular sessions between Malcolm and his wing probation officer were necessary over a two month period before any real trust could be established. Then, more purposeful work was agreed, looking at the impact of Malcolm's offending — first, on his family, then on his victims. He was taken back over a substantial criminal career to look at the process by which he got into trouble, the options he could have chosen — and the choices he would still have to make if Gina was to be convinced that he could change.

It was an uneven period. Good intentions are easy in prison but there is limited scope for demonstrating them. Malcolm wanted an early sign that Gina would reconsider; she would not provide this. Interviews varied between determination, despair and grudging cooperation, but gradually the two probation officers — inside and outside — and Malcolm and Gina moved towards a shared meeting to establish realistic plans for the future.

As part of this process, Malcolm began work in the specialist section of the prison workshops which produced Braille books. He found it unexpectedly absorbing and quickly became expert. Two visits from his children provided tangible proof — at last — of progress and it was clear that he was increasingly willing to reconsider his life and his future.

He will be released to independent accomodation at first. Gina is still understandably cautious about whether the changes will last. Supervision and counselling will pass to the outside probation officer, who says he expects the parole period to be "a bit of a rollercoaster". But the foundations for change were well laid, in prison; a good example of taking opportunities when they occur, which is a skill probation officers soon acquire.

Groupwork remains one of the most effective techniques employed in prisons. The national Sex Offender Treatment Programme builds on this and works to a set curriculum at a range of prisons, following pilot work in 1992. It is demanding, staff intensive, closely monitored and costly in resource terms—but it does offer the most coherent and sustained attempt to work positively with a particularly risky group of offenders.

The sheer scope of groupwork in prisons is often not realised. Drawing on other disciplines as well as probation, it may include:

- drug and alcohol groups—education and treatment as well as support for those who have completed a group
- anger management—particularly for prisoners whose offending is associated with loss of control
- men and violence—for prisoners who have used violence and bullying, but not in the context of loss of control
- offending behaviour programmes—often based on developing thinking and reasoning skills
- relationships counselling—dealing with past and current problems, as well as the inevitable adjustments which will have to be made on release
- money management—advice on finance, debt, and generally reconciling gross habits with net income
- pre-release groups—to look at immediate practical problems and survival strategies

The following description of a session at an alcohol education group, also taken from the 1996 Inspectorate report mentioned above gives some indication both of the skilled work that such groups require and of the results which can be achieved.

The group worked hard and they used a mixture of whole group and small group and individual exercises and it was clear that the men had already become involved in, interested in and affected by the material they had heard earlier in the week. The first few minutes of the group consisted of people reporting on homework they had done since the last session. It was clear that people were thinking in different ways about alcohol and their ability to control and make choices and the impact of alcohol on their lives. Most of the group were serious and worked hard and when they attempted to minimise their behaviour or blame others, were appropriately challenged. I was impressed by the way that in the small groups, almost without any direction, everybody participated. The staff moved around encouraging, questioning and assisting where they felt this was necessary. The whole tone of the group was one of considerable honesty with people describing fairly horrific crimes but more importantly describing with a great deal of feeling how much they had lied, cheated, been violent to people they cared about, particularly wives, in order to get out to drink. For example, several men commented that they caused rows deliberately in order to be able to storm out of the house because they wanted to go drinking or that they came in drunk and caused a row by criticising their wife in order that she would feel guilty rather than attack them. Staff constantly referred to the fact that the men needed to understand their feelings in addition to acknowledging their behaviour if they were to have a change in the future.

It was hard work, persistent and they kept the session going without a break for an hour and three-quarters after which they were going to have a break and continue. I left at that point. Overall, the group was very participatory, was good tempered, it was focused, everyone worked hard, it was well planned and all the leaders contributed and all the members participated. Once or twice I felt that they focused on one individual in front of the rest of the group and I wondered about the wisdom of that and sometimes they seemed to ask too many questions without giving a chance for people to think and respond. I would have wanted them to allow a bit more time. But generally my overall impression was of an extremely good group work programme and process.

ESTABLISHING CONTINUITY OF SUPERVISION

Prison sometimes exacerbates problems; sometimes helps resolve them, as the previous examples show. It's universal effect is to *delay* the chance to tackle, first hand, some of the problems in the community that every prisoner must face. It also imposes fresh hurdles—freedom brings extra difficulties in getting jobs or accommodation ('What have you been doing for the last six months?' is no longer an innocent question) or in trying to mend fractured relationships with partners, parents or children.

Sharing work in prison with the probation officer outside and sharing family contacts with those behind the wall therefore takes on a new impetus. It is difficult to overestimate the importance of this process, but there are many barriers to it:

96

- *distance:* all too often, prisoners are held a long way from the communities to which they are to return
- *movement:* unplanned movements often as a result of prison overcrowding or discipline problems make consistent work difficult
- *visits:* for both practical (workload and distance) and cost reasons, much less prison visiting by outside officers is now undertaken
- *systems:* feedback and information systems need to be much improved. There is no common record or file.

All these need continuing work but, despite uneven progress, work is being attempted which will bring about improvements.

DEALING WITH DISCRIMINATION

The issue of anti-discriminatory practice runs through the whole of probation work but is at its sharpest in prison. As a starting point it is worth remembering that, although only 5.5 per cent of the overall population come from minority ethnic groups, those same groups comprise some 18 per cent of all prisoners. This over-representation is not supported by data on offence seriousness—it can only be attributed to differential treatment: the use of remands in custody, the length and number of prison sentences, all show evidence of discrimination and unequal treatment. By way of comparison, 5.1 per cent of offenders on community penalties are from ethnic minority groups.

This background has sometimes been compounded by white probation staff working in prison, whose fear of making mistakes or giving offence has resulted in work that is stilted or, on occasion, unhelpful. Small wonder that black offenders in prison are often angry. Yet their very anger reinforces stereotypes about black people being arrogant or having chips on their shoulders.

Anti-racist practice is, simply, good practice. But it has to take account of the system within which it works and the anger of many prisoners from minority groups will not be easily overcome. Extra time and effort may be needed to form useful relationships in a prison setting, with good training, comprehensive racial monitoring to ensure non-discriminatory policies and practices (especially important with key documents like parole reports) and more involvement in the work by ethnic minority staff. All are important if the situation is to continue to improve.

THROUGHCARE

In 1993 the Prison and Probation Services, working in partnership, produced a joint document, *National Framework for the Throughcare of Offenders in Custody to the Completion of Supervision in the Community*. It remains the key document for implementing an effective throughcare[1] policy; the 'seamless sentence' already noted in the section on *Sentence Planning* earlier in this chapter. It lists in considerable detail the ways the two services need to work together if throughcare is to succeed, the roles of various staff groups, core tasks and even the model agreement by which the framework can be converted into action.

The section headed 'The Role of Seconded Probation Staff' is worth reproducing in full.

> The Prison Service has overall responsibility for throughcare whilst offenders are in custody and the Probation Service has overall responsibility when offenders are released. In order to assist in its throughcare task the Prison Service utilises the particular expertise of probation staff.
>
> Whether working with prisoners in the community or in prisons, probation staff bring to their respective throughcare roles a range of skills:

- skills in the assessment of dangerousness and risk, coupled with an appreciation of the surveillance/support structures necessary to reduce crime and to protect the public from sexual and other violent offenders
- skills in the identification and assessment of offenders' behaviour, motivation, and likely future behaviour, especially on return to the community
- skills in, and a body of knowledge about, various types of abnormal patterns of behaviour, e.g. addictive, compulsive, aggressive and violent
- experience and knowledge of the criminal justice system: roles of various agencies; powers of the courts; parole, experience gained through working relationships with judges, magistrates, police and the Crown Prosecution Service
- knowledge of the Family Courts structure and system, especially care procedures, divorce, parental responsibility, residence and contact
- knowledge of community resources and agency responsibilities, including specialist offender provision
- experience of licence supervision and throughcare systems
- skills in analysing behaviour pertinent to work with offenders in prison or the community, e.g. stigmatisation and discrimination, alienation, scapegoating and institutionalisation

- skills in using and evaluating different methods of intervention, such as groupwork programmes and special projects
- training in the use of social work methods: e.g. cognitive and social skills, individual and family counselling, therapeutic and problem-solving groupwork techniques, behaviour modification, conciliation and mediation
- report-writing skills
- training skills
- negotiation and inter-agency skills.

Seconded probation staff therefore have an essential role to play in helping prison establishments to provide effective throughcare'.

Despite overcrowding, financial pressures, reduced staff numbers and problems ranging from mentally disordered offenders to foreign nationals, the framework represents an ideal worth striving for. Throughcare, at its best, tries to make good use of time in prison, while never losing sight of the real world in waiting; later it tries to cope with the pressures of freedom while never forgetting the learning from prison. Progress towards delivering the national framework has been very uneven but, at least, it provides a focus for work which probation staff *should* be undertaking. Alongside are other important areas of work, particularly in relation to drugs, which are shared with other staff groups in prisons. The advent of mandatory drug testing of prisoners, drug free wings and special education and treatment programmes has recognised the seriousness of the issue as well as offering positive options for change.

The first edition of this book quoted a prison probation officer, Bill Cornwell;

> Do probation officers feel alien to the prison regime? I suppose they do. After all, the objectives of the prison in the current climate are simply to get a prisoner through his or her sentence without escaping and without committing suicide. Probation officers hope for more than that. Prison staff tend to look inwards, towards the centre of the prison, but probation officers look from the centre outwards. That is a fundamental difference which has always been there.

The impact of good, purposeful probation contact on prisoners cannot be isolated from the many other influences—often, but not exclusively harmful—that they experience in the course of a prison sentence. It is wrong, however, to see the work as mere damage limitation. Research evidence in both Britain and Europe has demonstrated the effectiveness of work inside prisons in delaying or reducing reoffending.

The 1998 Prisons and Probation Review identified enormous scope for better joint work and, even though the main focus will be on structural changes when the review reaches the decision stage, developing the joint agenda can only help the work of probation staff in prison. Chief officer staff from the probation service have been seconded to help promote this agenda for the future—it is the probation officer on the prison wing or houseblock who will have to put it into practice.

ENDNOTE

[1] The term 'throughcare' has been used in *Chapter 7* since it appears in all current documents. The home secretary has said, however, that he would like to see the term changed to something more appropriate and clear to the public. 'Resettlement' is the favoured replacement term—and is probably a real improvement.

CHAPTER 8

Release on Licence

For many years, the full title of the Probation Services of England and Wales was the 'Probation and *After Care* Service'—the title indicating, quite properly, the importance of work when offenders leave prison and have to come to terms, once more, with the real world. The origins of after care were charitable. Traditionally, when a man left prison his debt was paid and he was free of obligations or limits on his freedom. But the reality was that prison also fractured relationships, imposed social and psychological handicaps, made employment and accommodation more difficult and generally imposed a series of hurdles to independent living that many could not surmount.

Charitable bodies, often known as Discharged Prisoners Aid Societies, frequently came to the rescue, with help in terms of both cash and counselling. Gradually, as outlined in *Chapter 7*, the task grew to the extent that more formal arrangements were needed. Work in prisons became an integral part of the Probation Service's overall task in 1966; parole supervision was added two years later. (Post release arrangements for young offenders released from borstals had been a statutory duty since 1908). Now nearly all prisoners sentenced to 12 months or more are subject to supervision on release, and this forms an integral part of the sentence, not an optional extra. *Figure 1* (page 90) shows the post-release supervision arrangements which apply from January 1999 and the difference between some of these categories is explained more fully in the text.

For a service which had its origins in keeping offenders *out* of prison, the change to closer working has not always been easy, as indicated in the previous chapter. Nor has the development of work following release. For years it was accorded less status, priority and resources than court-ordered supervision and it has taken a combination of inspections, National Standards and much hard work to try to restore the balance. The reasons are, perhaps, obvious. Men released from prison were likely to be much less co-operative than those who had recently agreed a contract with the court; ex-prisoners often blamed their probation officers for the prison sentence, anyway; sanctions were slow and uncertain and the problems faced by many ex-prisoners made purposeful supervision very difficult indeed.

Change has been slow and the feeling that after care is really only intended to undo the damage the prison has inflicted will not disappear, simply because it retains an uncomfortable amount of truth. But two key factors have helped to produce a broader view, the introduction of parole (now discretionary conditional release) for prisoners serving *longer* sentences; and the expansion of post-release supervision for those serving *shorter* terms (automatic conditional release): see page 90.

Discretionary conditional release

The scheme of what used, quite properly, to be called 'parole' and which is now, by statute, termed 'discretionary conditional release' (DCR) has changed somewhat in recent years. But the essential elements remain the same—the early release of selected prisoners serving *longer* sentences of four years and over subject to careful assessment and strict licence conditions, with recall to prison through the Parole Board (which remains), not the courts (other than where a fresh offence is committed). DCR is often still called 'parole' by practitioners and prisoners.

Although parole/DCR provides the same opportunities as other forms of licence, it has always seemed qualitatively different, and has been supervised with considerable care—and equally considerable success.

Over 90 per cent of such supervision cases are usually completed successfully. The feeling that the sentence is still being served, albeit in the community, is certainly part of the reason; the other may lie in the selection process. There has always been a tension between the needs of individuals and those of the overall scheme. It was important for the scheme to succeed in the early days, so only the good-risk prisoners were released on licence. Yet it is the bad-risk prisoners, who would otherwise be released later without any supervision at all, who might need the period of contact most if reconviction risks are to be reduced. With increasing confidence from a number of years of successful operation, the Parole Board began to widen the scope, but the balance between risk and need is still a difficult one. These are, by definition, some of the most serious offenders. The selection process also made comparative research difficult; the best evidence from a matched pair study suggests that parole has a successful *short term* effect (the licence period) and a smaller, but significant, effect on criminal behaviour during the two years following release. Supervision by probation officers, it was clear, *did* make a difference and the Probation Service responded with enthusiasm.

DCR is considered further later in this chapter.

102

Automatic conditional release

The second factor was the expansion of post-release supervision for shorter sentences. 'Short term' prisoners (those serving 12 months but less than four years) are released on 'automatic conditional release' (ACR) after serving half their sentence and are supervised until the three-quarters point.

Supervision periods for those on ACR are thus short (a 16 month sentence would include eight months in prison and four months on licence) and good sentence planning can mean that it is purposeful and effective—the notion of the 'seamless sentence', with its aim that work before, during and after the period in prison should have a clear and realistic focus on the issues that were crucial to offending behaviour in the first place, underpins this model and the National Standards (see next section) reinforce it.

ACR is considered further later in this chapter.

GENERAL ARRANGEMENTS

Some points apply to all types of release. Overall, the reality of release on licence is best captured by the relevant National Standards.

National Standards

The overall aims of the *National Standards for Supervision Before and After Release from Custody* are set out in the relevant standards. They are:

* the rehabilitation of the offender
* the protection of the public from harm from the offender
* the prevention of further offending.

Central to all of these is the management of risk and public protection. Risk assessment (not just of reoffending but of suicide or self-harm, or to staff) is a continuing process and needs to be reviewed at regular intervals. Work within the prison has already been covered in *Chapter 7*; joint work with the 'through care' officer is likely to centre on five tasks:

* *minimising personal deterioration:* keeping a realistic view of the world outside, encouraging links, and above all, encouraging some reflection on attitudes to offending
* *sustaining family links:* not least because, if they are fractured, the risks of reoffending are much greater
* *preparing realistic release plans:* whether it is help with accommodation, employment, state benefits or social contacts

- *pre-release or home circumstances reports:* which give the prison or the Parole Board vital information before decisions are made about suitability for release or home detention curfews
- *victim work:* this relatively new responsibility on probation services is covered in more detail later in this chapter.

The National Standards, rightly, put considerable emphasis on early contact following release—a first interview at the probation office on the day of release, or—if unavoidable—on the next working day and a home visit within five working days of the first interview. A second interview, following which the supervision plan should be finalised, should take place within ten working days of release. For this is a crucial period, and not just because of an understandable desire to celebrate new found freedoms in the pub or elsewhere. Quite apart from practical problems, families have made adjustments to loss—and suddenly have to receive the prisoner back in their midst. People have changed, children have grown up. New friends, skills and relationships have altered an equation during a period when time has often stood still for a prisoner. Being sensitive to this, and dealing with the problems it produces, is often a key task in supervision following release.

Threats to post-release licence
There are two factors, in particular, which may yet undermine post-release licence supervision. Sheer numbers, from a burgeoning and apparently inexorable rise in the prison population, are one. They threaten to swamp the system, which is already dangerously stretched and the experience of custody, where many constructive programmes have withered in the last few years (a dual problem of overcrowding and security), is not of a seamless sentence, with purposeful work in prison; all too often it is of an aimless period with easy access to drugs. The second is electronic monitoring—the tagging of prisoners for up to two months in advance of their expected release date. More details of this are given in the section on probation and electronic tagging in *Chapter 11*; the impact on licence supervision is the issue here. If supervision becomes more mechanical; more reliant on technology than careful risk assessment, then we shall lose some of the real gains that have been made in recent years.

The language has also changed over the years, from 'after care' to 'through care' (to reinforce the continuity of work) to 'licence' (to reinforce the point that the sentence is still being served, albeit in the community).

SPECIAL CASES AND CONSIDERATIONS

So far, I have considered issues which apply to all prisoners regardless of sentence length. The two main categories—automatic conditional release and discretionary conditional release—do have some differences and are worth considering separately. Before turning to this, some other exceptions to the general arrangements are also worth noting.

Sexual and violent offenders
Sexual or violent offenders may be subject to a specially extended period of post-release supervision—which can extend to the whole of the sentence term—if the court considers this necessary to protect the public.

Lifers
Life sentence prisoners continue to be on licence indefinitely, but the period of actual supervision may be terminated, with the agreement of the Parole Board when it no longer seems to serve a useful purpose. A gradually reducing level of supervision may be necessary over several years before the decision is finally made.

Young offenders
Young offenders are *all* subject to three months supervision if they are serving less than 12 months, provided this does not take them beyond their twenty second birthday.

Special considerations affecting ACR
These cases—covering sentences of one to four years—require a pre-discharge report to be sent by the supervision officer to the prison, one month before release. Reports must cover the verified address to which the prisoner will go on release; where appropriate, the family's attitude towards his or her homecoming; work prospects; other local factors (the local community's attitude, the influence of associates or issues relating to the victim) and a tentative release plan. In cases where there may be a risk to children, confirmation is needed that social services departments have been consulted about supervision post-release in order to protect future potential victims.

As with other forms of supervision, the requirements need to be fully and carefully explained and the supervision plan jointly drawn up. Short periods of licence concentrate the mind wonderfully—realistic, task centred work that enables a real sense of achievement to be gained are much preferable to grander plans which are unlikely to be realised in the time available.

If the conditions of the order are not kept, breaches of the licence are prosecuted in the magistrates' court and the supervising officer has to adhere to the requirements of the Police and Criminal Evidence Act of 1984 in terms of process. This may change—the Crime and Disorder Act 1998 makes provision to transfer the responsibility for recalling short term prisoners to the Parole Board—but current information suggests that it may be some time before this is implemented. In either case, a report is needed covering:

- the offender's response to supervision before and after the instigation of breach action
- an explanation for the breach
- an assessment of risk, and
- a recommendation about how reasonable it would be for the offender to continue under supervision, be fined, returned to prison or dealt with by any other sentencing option.

Special considerations affecting DCR
General principles apply with these more serious and longer term cases, too, but there may be more stringent conditions of licence and liability to recall to prison. Additional conditions (theoretically possible for all licensees but more likely with DCR) may cover:

- medical or psychiatric help
- a prohibition on certain work or voluntary activity (risks attached to some sex offenders are obviously paramount here)
- prohibitions on contact with named prisoners
- requirements concerning approved living arrangements.

In addition to any breach of licence conditions, the supervising officer has also to take account of:

- situations where the offender's behaviour is such that further serious offences are likely to be committed
- grounds for believing that the safety of the public may for any reason be at risk
- the possibility of the offender's behaviour bringing the licence system into disrepute, or impeding supervision activity.

These clearly represent the sharp edge of risk management in terms of dealing with potential, rather than actual, behaviour. When liberty is at stake, too, there need to be reasonable safeguards against any abuse of power. Consequently, any proposal for recall by a probation officer supervising a discretionary release case has to be approved by an assistant chief probation officer before being submitted, in writing, to the Parole Board. Lesser breaches can be dealt with by way of a formal warning letter.

The Parole Board, which considers all cases for discretionary release as well as recommendations for recall, consists of a mixture of professional and lay people with an interest in, or connection to, the criminal justice process. Judges, psychiatrists, criminologists and chief probation officers are all well represented and cases are considered by panels designed to ensure a spread of interests. A small group of civil servants provides administrative support. The parole process requires that prisoners are given reasons if parole is denied and this has to be done with care and sensitivity, since it may be as a result of information given in the home circumstances report prepared by the probation service.

MAKING A DIFFERENCE?

Is post-release supervision really any different to any other kind of court order, once the technical differences over recall, breach and special conditions are taken into account? Certainly much of the approach is the same and of course many of the problems are identical. Finding work, with a criminal record, for instance, may be equally problematic whether you have just left court or custody.

Yet there *are* some differences of approach which I think remain important. 'Through care' implies a real concern for an individual throughout his or her sentence, and that means taking contact seriously even when the offender is safely tucked away in prison. Distance and other pressures often mean that visiting may be a rarity but telephone contact, links with the prison probation officer and—above all—that much undervalued communication, the letter, mean that a basis of trust and co-operation can be established well before the date of release. It will certainly pay dividends afterwards. Good links with the prison probation officer are equally important, as is any family work that can be accomplished during sentence.

Supervision after release has come a very long way from its charitable and humanitarian beginnings. One objective—to help in the continuing rehabilitative process—may be the same but self interest on the part of society (in reducing reoffending) and the needs of an integrated sentence—part prison based, part served in the community—are important, too.

107

WORK WITH VICTIMS

Until recently, work with victims did not figure in the statutory responsibilities of the probation service. This was not because of a lack of interest—individual probation officers had not only been closely associated with the setting up of local victim support schemes, but had maintained important links in terms of joint training, support and ongoing work. Many probation areas, too, ensured that a victim perspective was included in work with offenders, to ensure that they were aware of the impact of the offence on the victim and the consequences.

My own service used carefully selected victims to join groups of young offenders who had committed burglaries. The victim was able to say, simply and forcefully, what it felt like to find their home and possessions violated, the feeling of insecurity and the anxieties which followed. Equally, in a Kent prison, a group of long sentence prisoners convicted of robbery offences would meet, over several weeks, a bank cashier and a petrol station attendant who had been robbed and who knew at first hand the terror and trauma involved. Both groups had a profound effect on offenders, whose initial denial and excuses ('It was only the insurance company that lost out') were cut short by the process of coming to face-to-face with the effects of their actions.

Despite small scale initiatives, however, and despite the enormous amount of invaluable work undertaken every year by Victim Support there was still a feeling that victims were the unheard voice of the criminal justice process and that probation officers were much too focused on offenders and their welfare.

The first step towards righting that balance came with the publication of the *Victims Charter* in 1990, which gave specific responsibilities to criminal justice agencies to provide services to victims of crime.

Now, probation services have a duty to victims of violent or sexual offences, where the offender has been sentenced to more than four years imprisonment. That responsibility is two-fold:

- first, to provide information to the victim shortly after sentence. This should happen within two months, although it is clear that, for some victims, a longer period following the court process is more appropriate. Information is given on:

  — the details of the sentence
  — the offender's likely progress in prison
  — how decisions are made about early release

— the safeguards that exist after an offender is released
— other sources of support, especially through victim support schemes.

- second, for victims who wish it, to keep in touch and re-visit when early release decisions are being considered, to ensure that any concerns they have can be passed on to the prison authorities, and taken into account when release decisions are being made.

The reaction of victims to this new service has been overwhelmingly positive. Some had no information on the sentence passed, others no idea about likely progress and possible release, especially if the offender would be living locally. Comments have included:

> I had no idea whether he was still in prison. You hear all sorts of rumours. I dreaded going out in case I saw him around, although I am not sure I would recognise him, as it has been 17 years since he killed my daughter.

> I want the Parole Board to know what the attack really meant to me. It is good to know that someone will listen to this, even if it doesn't affect the sentence.

Many probation areas have specialist staff to undertake this work, but all probation officers should experience it—an awareness of victim issues and experiences will enhance supervision practice, improve the quality of pre-sentence reports and help to make sense of events that sometimes prove difficult for both offender and victim. The work demands real sensitivity, an awareness of who *can* provide help to victims who need it—and it frequently contains surprises.

I recently undertook victim liaison visits to two building society cashiers, both in their twenties, who had been held at knifepoint in a robbery at a local branch. Each had experienced the knife only inches from their throat, held by a man desperate for money to buy heroin. Neither, fortunately, had been physically harmed. It had taken 14 months for the case to be disposed of at the Crown Court, when a five year sentence had been passed, and I really didn't know what to expect when I set out for the two home visits.

At the first, I found Julie, an extrovert and articulate character. She had a few questions abut the sentence passed but had no other concerns. She had returned to work the following day, had helped the building society in designing security improvements and, while appreciating our interest, saw no reason to keep in touch. It had been pretty awful on the day, she agreed, but she looked on it as a comparable risk to a nasty accident if, for instance, she had to drive in the course of her work.

The second victim, Carla, could not have been more different. Still haunted by the experience, she had experienced periods of depression, of being afraid to leave the house, and of recurring nightmares. She had only just returned to work and still felt fearful of almost anyone who came in. The building society had offered her counselling (just two sessions, it appeared) but she felt there was little sympathy, now, from her employers or her husband. 'No one actually says it' she said, with a wan smile 'but what they *want* to say is 'Pull yourself together'. And if I could, I would . . . '. This became the first of several visits, with a focus on whether the offender would return locally (he did not, having secured a place at a drug rehabilitation centre some 150 miles away) and how she could find some ongoing help. The local Victim Support group provided this over a three month period—fortunately, with some real success.

Some victims want to meet their offender, if he was previously unknown to them. 'Why me?' is the question they want answered, but it is also about understanding the genesis of the offence, knowing whether fears are realistic—and seeing the human face behind a deliberately impersonal process. Such meetings can only take place with consent on both sides and even then need skilled and sensitive handling. But they can have positive and sometimes dramatic results. One recent case concerned a woman who lived alone and whose garage had been set on fire by a young man. A serious tragedy had only been avoided when a neighbour promptly called the fire brigade. He had eventually received a six year sentence for arson and a number of burglary offences but, having offered a guilty plea and only the sketchiest of statements Mrs Carroll, the victim, was left wondering about almost everything connected with her offence. She asked to meet Graham, the offender, in prison; after some negotiation, the probation officer agreed to arrange it. It wasn't only "Why me?"' said Mrs Carroll

> I had seen him in the dock and he could have been one of my nephews. Why had he been in my garage? Why set fire to it? I needed to *understand* what had been going on if I was to feel safe in future. All I'd been able to do up to then was keep the garage door locked.

Graham was just as nervous as Mrs Carroll when the meeting started— indeed, both looked terrified as they sat down in the prison visits cubicle. But there was no doubting the sincerity of Graham's blurted apology which started things off—and he had also written it down so

Mrs Carroll could take it away. The story was, perhaps, predictable. Graham had become dependant on drugs—'anything I could smoke, or swallow, or inject', he said ruefully—and supported his habit with the proceeds of walk-in burglaries. He had seen the open door of Mrs Carroll's garage and slid in to see what he could steal. There was nothing of any value but he was conscious that he might have been seen, knew his fingerprints were everywhere and thought a fire would cover his tracks . . .

He had been appalled by the destruction, too, but had been too befuddled to even think about the consequences.

The interview was 'probably the most useful hour's meeting I've ever organized—for both of them' according to the probation officer. 'Mrs Carroll knows there was nothing personal—her house was chosen at random, in a street Graham had never visited before. He feels he can put the offence—and his guilt—behind him. She can sleep a good deal more safely at night'.

Mediation of this order is unusual, but has a real role to play. More widely, work with victims may help them recover; it certainly helps to reduce the fear of crime and has a real impact on individual offenders. There can be few more important contributions, even if small scale, to community safety.

111

CHAPTER 9

Youth Justice

Few topics raise as much concern, both public and political, as juvenile and youth justice.[1] It was at the top of the agenda when the new Labour government started work in May 1997 and much of what follows in this chapter stems from the work of the Youth Justice Task Force, the consultation paper *No More Excuses: A New Approach to Tackling Youth Crime in England and Wales* (Cmnd. 3809, November 1997); and the legislation which followed in the Crime and Disorder Act 1998. Some radical, innovative (and controversial) new measures will be tested in the next few years, under the auspices of the new National Youth Justice Board and the success or failure of these measures will have a profound effect on the work of the probation service. Despite the fact that the overall impact of youth crime is limited in resource terms— because the work is shared with other, and usually larger, agencies— today's young juvenile offenders will, all too soon, be the young adult offenders of tomorrow if effective work is not undertaken. There are still many opportunities for probation officers to engage in direct work with young offenders and these are likely to increase; this, too, reinforces the importance of understanding the changes which will transform the youth justice system.

JUVENILE COURTS AND YOUTH COURTS

Some background and history is helpful. Parliament first ensured that young people should be kept separate from adult offenders, and treated differently, by establishing juvenile courts in the Children Act of 1908. That Act, too, started the process, which continued in the following half century, of trying to ensure that the *welfare principle* underpinned work with children and young people; there was also the principle of avoiding the use of the criminal courts altogether which was seen as a desirable aim in some circumstances.

Originally, the juvenile courts had jurisdiction over children aged eight to 15. Later the age of criminal responsibility was raised to ten and the upper limit to 17. The term youth court has been used since 1992 when the upper age limit was also raised to 18.

Youth court magistrates are appointed to a youth court panel (from the wider group who also serve in the adult courts: special arrangements exist in London where magistrates are appointed direct to the panel) and receive special training. This emphasises the difference between offending by adults and young people—the recognition of immaturity, the fact that many young people pass through a difficult stage in their lives and may well challenge or test out authority. Crime by young people is not something unusual which sets them apart— Home Office research shows that, among 14-25 year olds one in two males and one in three females admits to having committed an offence—and many 'grow out of crime' as they get older and experience the satisfactions and responsibilities of adult life.

That being so, prosecution may often *not* be needed. Informal warnings and official police cautions are frequently and effectively used to avoid the use of court proceddings and the handicap of a formal criminal record. Where prosecution was necessary, the duty of the juvenile court was clearly laid down in the Children and Young Persons Act 1933:

> Every court in dealing with a child or young person who is brought before it, either as an offender or otherwise, shall have regard to the welfare of the child or young person, and shall in a proper case take steps for removing him from undesirable surroundings, and for security that proper provision is made for his education and training.

In this context a 'child' is (now) aged 10-13 years inclusive and a 'young person' from 14 to 17 years inclusive.

Over the years, the sentencing powers of the youth court have been made more flexible and designed specifically for a younger age group. The use of custody has been made subject to very specific criteria and the supervision order (the young person's equivalent to the probation order) broadened to try and take account of the needs of young people.

The supervision order may be made for up to three years, and supervised by a local authority social worker, a probation officer or any member of one of the new inter-agency Young Offender Teams (normally called YOTs) which have been developed and are now set to become the basic structure for all youth justice work. The order can cover a wide range of requirements:

- to live at a particular place
- to attend at a specified place at specified times
- to take part in various forms of activity (including very intensive programmes of supervised activity)
- to remain at home for specified periods between 6 p.m. and 6 a.m.
- to refrain from taking part in particular activities
- to receive psychiatric treatment
- to attend school or follow other educational arrangements

• to live in local authority accommodation for a specified period of up to six months.

THE ROLE OF THE PROBATION SERVICE

Juvenile courts traditionally dealt with much more than crime—truancy and failure to attend school, care orders and place of safety orders and adoption. There was thus a multi-agency approach to serving the courts, with social workers and education welfare officers also involved and probation officers concentrating largely on crime. Changes in 1969 (which allowed supervision to be undertaken by local authority social workers *or* probation officers) and in 1989 (which took all civil matters to a new family proceedings courts) gradually provided a much sharper focus, but the probation service role varied enormously in different parts of the country. Some probation areas had no involvement at all in the youth court—agreement was reached with the relevant social services department that it should take over the work, consistent with their more general duties and responsibilities towards children and young people. Other Probation Services agreed demarcation lines— social services would take all those up to a certain point (14, 15 or 16 years of age, depending on local negotiations), leaving probation officers to deal with the older age range. A smaller group created local inter-agency arrangements, in which multi-disciplinary YOTs dealt with all the work coming from the courts and using resources from police, social services and probation; and from education and youth and community departments, too.

YOTs have been influential in pointing the way towards a much more integrated service for young people in trouble—Hampshire, Kent and Northamptonshire have been particularly active in promoting their use—and future provision, which will involve all probation areas, builds on their experience.

THE 'PROBLEM' OF YOUTH CRIME

The 1970s and 1980s saw significant changes in the approach to youth crime:

• *intermediate treatment (IT)* schemes—usually a form of intensive activity-based supervision—attracted considerable funds to offer imaginative programmes of help, treatment and developmental work to young people

Youth Justice

- *court diversion schemes* replicated many of these, pre-court, as a way of keeping young people out of the formal court system altogether.

Voluntary bodies, such as the Rainer Foundation, Fairbridge and the National Children's Home became partners in schemes to provide everything from adventure camps to residential facilities and community projects.

There was some disquiet and criticism of the non-punitive approach, which many felt had gone too far. 'Treats for tearaways' and 'goodies for baddies' were frequently quoted as evidence that the system had gone soft on crime. Yet the results were impressive—a decrease from 7,400 to 1,400 between 1980-1992 in the number of young people under 17 in custody, and a huge drop in the use of care orders made in criminal proceedings (from 2,700 to 100) in the same period.

But both the statistics and public and political attitudes began to change, especially in the early 1990s. Highly publicised cases of prolific, multiple offending, especially 'joy riding' and burglary, repeat offending on bail and the tragic murder of toddler Jamie Bulger in 1992 by two ten year olds were all significant. The move to 'toughen up' sentencing for young people was already under way when several reported cases of young offenders being sent on expensive trips abroad were used to tighten the screw still further.

The problems are real. About 42 per cent of indictable crime seems to be committed by people aged under 21, with 25 per cent of known offenders aged under 18 and 17 per cent aged 18-20. The numbers have, however, fallen in recent years:

1996	1995	1986
124,100	132,800	176,000

Numbers of offenders aged 10-17 cautioned/found guilty of indictable offences

The 1996 figure represents a fall of six per cent from the previous year and nearly 30 per cent from a decade earlier. Expressed in terms of the numbers of young offenders found guilty or cautioned for indictable offences per 100,00 of population, the figures are as follows:

1986	1996	
2,527	1,365	for boys aged 10-13
762	551	for girls aged 10-13
7,148	6,164	for boys aged 14-17
1,578	1,647	for girls aged 14-17

Only the last of these shows an increase; in some areas, such as the 46 per cent drop in boys aged 10-13 who have offended, the decline seems to have been remarkable. But it was reported in a Home Office bulletin concerning its *Criminal Statistics* for 1995 that there seemed to have been an increase in the use by police of *informal* warnings to young offenders, so the substantial falls shown above might well be accounted for, in part, by this. However, we do know that the peak age for offenders was, for many years prior to 1988, 15 for both boys and girls. With the changes shown above it is now 18 for boys and 15 for girls.

Cautioning rates do still vary considerably. For example:

		Highest cautioning rate	Lowest cautioning rate
Boys aged	10-13	96%	72%
		(Suffolk)	(Northamptonshire)
	14-17	74%	32%
		(Norfolk)	(Durham)

But results suggest that, overall, cautioning is still very effective. Only 18 per cent of offenders cautioned in 1994 were convicted of a standard list offence within two years of the caution. It is second or subsequent cautions which are much less likely to be successful.

Most of these young people, in fact, commit only one or two offences while growing up. But a small hard core of persistent offenders have a disproportionate effect. Home Office research has found that only three per cent of young offenders account for 26 per cent of youth crime. Although most are property crimes, known offending rates for both robbery and drug offences have also, worryingly, increased.

Although there is no easy link of cause and effect in relation to youth crime, the range of risk factors (psychological, family, social, economic and cultural) and the correlation with social disadvantage and poverty are well known. The key factors related to youth criminality are:

- being male
- being brought up by a criminal parent or parents
- living in a family with multiple problems
- poor parenting and lack of supervision
- poor discipline in the family or at school

- truancy or exclusion from school
- associating with delinquent friends, and
- having siblings who offend.

(*Young People and Crime:* Home Office Research Study 145)

The single most important factor is the quality of a young persons home life, including parental supervision. (As with adults, the bulk of youth crime is committed by males. In 1996, 142,600 males aged 10-17 were convicted or cautioned; the figure for young females was 34,400. For both, the risk of becoming serious or persistent offenders becomes higher the earlier the age someone starts committing offences).

Misspent youth

Criticism of the response to youth crime has centred on three aspects. First, the perceived conflict between the welfare of the young person and the need to protect the public, punish offences and prevent reoffending. Overall, this should not be too large a stumbling block but individual cases do produce real dichotomies and the result has certainly been a loss of confidence in the system. Second, the problems of delay in dealing with cases; and third the adequacy of sanctions if the young person did not comply with the court order.

All three were addressed in *Misspent Youth,* an influential Audit Commission report (1996). They added other, equally serious, concerns of their own—that not enough was done to tackle offending behaviour, that the several agencies involved were often working in a very unco-ordinated way and that too little preventative work was being undertaken.

Most of the £1 billion spent on dealing with youth offenders, it said, was spent on processing and administration. Performance had little, if anything, to do with the level of resources and while there were examples of good practice they were difficult to spread. The different agencies—social services, education, probation—were accountable to different government departments; in short, it was a mess.

The Audit Commission's follow-up report in 1998, which used a series of local audits to produce an updated picture prior to the introduction of new legislation, was hardly more encouraging. Cases were still taking, on average, 4.5 months from arrest to sentence, with—typically—over two months before the case even got to court. Only two per cent of offenders were being given 'caution plus' programmes (a short programme of intervention with a formal caution, rather than a court hearing) despite the fact that these would soon be introduced nationally as 'warnings'. Only 30 per cent of youth justice workers time was being spent dealing directly with offending behaviour; information and monitoring systems were inadequate and educational needs of young people on supervision were not being properly dealt with.

The frustration of an unco-ordinated, wasteful and often very ineffective system was all too apparent. But the Audit Commission could also point to some very good practice on which to build, including 'fast-tracking' schemes, bail support programmes and joint work with schools. New legislation has therefore produced a comprehensive blueprint for the whole of the country covering:

- a new structure
- new penalties and interventions.

These, together with improved arrangements for existing powers, will provide the framework for work by probation staff and are therefore dealt with in more detail.

THE NEW FRAMEWORK

The Youth Justice Task Force proposed that the aim of preventing offending by young people should be achieved by the following objectives:

- swift justice—delays in the system to be greatly reduced
- confronting young offenders with the *consequences* of their offending—for themselves, their family, the victim and the community
- punishment proportionate to the seriousness and persistence of offending
- encouraging reparation to victims
- reinforcing the responsibilities of parents, and
- helping young offenders to tackle problems associated with their offending and to develop a sense of personal responsibility.

To translate this into reality a new National Youth Justice Board will oversee the new arrangements. There is now a statutory duty on local authorities, primarily through social services and education departments; and a statutory obligation on health authorities, the police and Probation Services; to establish Youth Offending Teams (YOTs) and to work to published annual Youth Justice Plans.

Such plans, which will have to fit with wider community safety plans, Children's Services Plans, and the business plans of all the agencies involved, will include set targets by central government. The aim is clearly for a much more consistent approach to youth justice and

118

a much more focused one. The range of new measures, together with existing powers, are shown in *Figure 2* and represent a sea-change, the effects of which will not be known for some years.

Within this framework, probation officers seconded to work in YOTs will be expected to:

- assess and manage the risk of reoffending
- make assessments and deliver interventions in support of the new 'final warning' scheme
- provide bail information and support services
- prepare pre-sentence reports for the youth court
- supervise community sentences including reparation orders
- make arrangements for the supervision of parenting orders and child safety orders
- provide through-care and post release supervision services for young people in custody

There are real reservations about some of the new orders and their potential on already disadvantaged young people. Equally, the practicability of some measures like local curfews and parenting orders has yet to be tested. Much will depend on the good common sense of youth panels and re-constituted youth courts.

But it will be an exciting time to be working in the youth justice field. Despite fears about the levels of resourcing, the opportunities offered by genuine inter-agency partnerships are enormous and exploiting these to provide a more coherent and effective response to youth crime is a real challenge—and opportunity.

Developments in this country, interestingly, mirror very closely the National Juvenile Justice Plan developed in the USA by attorney general Janet Reno. In her foreword to the plan (March 1996), which described the problem of juvenile crime as a national crisis, she wrote:

> Co-operative partnerships among justice, health, child welfare, education and social service systems can lay the foundation for measurable successes. Communities can generate solutions . . . individuals and groups can prevent or reduce violence in their own block or neighbourhood. The solutions are within reach. We can promote early intervention and prevention of youth violence. Together, we can redeem the promise that every young life holds.

Learning from either side of the Atlantic should prove a fascinating experience over the next few years.

1.	REPRIMAND	Administered by police. First offences only.
2.	CHILD SAFETY ORDER	Children under 10. Via family proceedings court
3.	CHILD CURFEW	Joint application by police/local authority. Children up to 10. 90 days max.
4.	FINAL WARNING	Replaces caution for second, or more serious offences. Includes intervention programme, supervised by YOTs
5.	ABSOLUTE OR CONDITIONAL DISCHARGE	Existing powers
6.	PARENTAL BIND-OVER	Existing powers
7.	FINE	Parents may also be fined
8.	COMPENSATION	As now: may be used in conjunction with new reparation order
9.	ACTION PLAN ORDER	New community penalty — short and intensive mix of punishment and help
10.	PARENTING ORDER	Programme of counselling and guidance for parents whose children truant or are subject to anti-social behaviour order
11.	REPARATION ORDER	Reparation in kind — up to 24 hours work, within 3 months
12.	ATTENDANCE CENTRE ORDER	
13.	SUPERVISION ORDER	Existing powers strengthened
14.	PROBATION ORDER	Offenders aged 16 or 17 only
15.	COMMUNITY SERVICE ORDER	Offenders aged 16 or 17 only
16.	COMBINATION ORDER	Mix of probation and community service: 16/17 year olds only
17.	CUSTODIAL REMANDS	Court may now direct the use of local authority 'secure accommodation' for all 12-14 year olds, 15-16 year old girls and 'vulnerable' 15-16 year old boys
18.	DETENTION AND TRAINING ORDER	New custodial sentence for 10-17 year olds served in 'secure accommodation'. If under 15, 'persistent offenders' only; if under 12, used only if needed to protect the public.
19.	SECTION 53 ORDER	(Children and Young Persons Act 1933) for the most serious offences only, e.g. murder, manslaughter, arson, rape
NOTE:		'secure accommodation' may be — a youth offender institution — a secure training centre — local authority secure accommodation
Implementation		3 and 13 from October 1998 17 from November 1998 1, 2, 4, 9, 10, 11 Pilot schemes from 30. 9. 1998

Youth Court Powers and Associated Measures
Following Crime and Disorder Act 1998

Figure 2

WORKING WITH YOUNG PEOPLE

The new range of measures available are, to say the least, comprehensive. The danger is that they are implemented in ways which forget that the young people involved are children first and young offenders second. A useful report published by the Scottish Office in February 1998 makes this point in its title—*Children, Young People and Offending*—and argues very effectively for the problems to be tackled early and the underlying causes addressed. The key action areas are not new, but set out a clear agenda of tried and tested policies:

• to reduce social exclusion, truancy, and bullying
• to promote nursery education and parental support
• to improve educational standards
• to develop effective and well-evaluated approaches to persistent offenders.

The last of these is where the distinctive contribution of probation staff in YOTs can most obviously be targeted but the Audit Commission described a more comprehensive agenda:

> Any strategy for tackling youth crime must consider how to address the behaviour of four different groups of young people. Targeting persistent offenders to get them to change their behaviour could have a significant effect on the overall level of youth crime. Young offenders who have yet to develop an entrenched pattern of offending must also be dealt with effectively and first-time offenders must also be discouraged from becoming more deeply involved in crime. Finally, young people at risk must be discouraged from being involved in the first place.
>
> *Misspent Youth*, 1996

Within this framework a wide variety of imaginative schemes have developed, many in parallel with schemes and programmes which have been found to work with older age groups. Cognitive-behavioural approaches (i.e. those aimed at changing behaviour beliefs and thought processes) underpin much groupwork; equally, activity based work has proved to be very successful and a number of partnerships are based on ensuring access to facilities of this kind, for example:

• in Wales, six probation services work alongside the Duke of Edinburgh Award Scheme, offering involvement in the bronze, silver and gold awards to young offenders aged over 14. The Personal Challenge programmes often focus on crime and delinquency and provide a real opportunity, with local community support, to set legitimate and positive objectives for the young offender's development

- Fairbridge, a national charity, offers personal development and adventure training through its urban-based centres. Small groups, often referred through YOTs, learn basic climbing and canoeing skills in 'taster' courses, along with personal and social skills which have a wider application. These may be used in expeditions and on-going training, as well as longer courses at the Venture Trust, a Home Office financed base in the mountain wilderness of Scotland. Inter-dependence, especially when you are dangling at the end of a rope, is a powerful message; so, too, are the dynamics of a group, whether on expeditions, co-operative cooking arrangements or group exercises. Fairbridge exploits these to the full and adds its own unique extra ingredient which I can only describe as 'stickability'. Staff keep in touch sometimes long after a supervision order has finished, to offer help with vocational training or employment, family problems—anything which is getting in the way of sustained progress. The long term results are impressive.

The Home Office is sponsoring research into a range of physical activities, and their impact in terms of supervision and eventual outcomes, but Young Offender Teams need access to a much wider range of provision. Working with young people needs a clear focus on their welfare but may also need to encompass:

- sustained work with parents and other family members
- particular links with schools—bullying, truancy or school exclusion may all have a dramatic impact
- special adolescent facilities, drug and alcohol advice, help with the use of leisure time
- health and hygiene advice and social skills.

Homework clubs, football teams, work experience placements, auto-offending groups, parenting classes, junior firefighting awards, environmental groups and mentoring schemes have all been organized and used by Young Offender Teams as ways of getting alongside and influencing young people. Mentors, in particular, offer a particularly valuable service; a concerned adult in the young person's community, giving time, interest and individual skills to help a troubled young person into adulthood, too.

Two other approaches are particularly worthy of note:

- *the Northamptonshire Diversion Unit* works with offenders aged ten and upwards with two main aims: to put right the harm created by crime and to prevent further offending. It deals with over 600 youth offenders each year and six different organizations, including police, probation, health and local authority services jointly fund and staff the unit. It operates a pre-prosecution scheme, hence the aim of diversion from formal court proceedings. Staff from the unit visit each offender *and* the victim and draw up an agreed plan aimed at preventing reoffending and putting right the offence. Both victims and offenders express a high level of satisfaction with the arrangements, which are also very cost effective.

- *Family Group Conferencing* is an older idea, with its roots in Maori culture, which stressed the ability of family and friends, rather than more formal structures, to resolve problems. The Australians added the principle of 'restorative justice' (adding the victim's right to be involved in the process and to receive satisfaction) before the model was translated to the youth justice system here. The Hampshire Youth Justice Service (Probation Service and Social Services Departments) have taken the lead in UK development. A co-ordinator arranges a special conference in appropriate cases. The young person's family members, the victim, the police and other significant adults such as youth workers or teachers all gather together to work out a realistic action plan which is acceptable to all parties. Police administer a caution rather than proceed to a formal court appearance and the various agencies continue to provide support, as the action plan is followed through.

Fairly elaborate arrangements of this kind cannot be made available to all offenders, of course, and much of the skill of YOT probation officers lies in assessing *which* programme or court sentence is most appropriate in an individual case. Supervision plans need to be clear and well understood; family support mobilised and use made of schools and other agencies if effective supervision of young people is to be sustained. The transition from childhood to adult life has always posed problems—higher expectations, fewer jobs, drugs and drink simply add to the hazards. All too many young offenders are themselves victims of poor parenting, inadequate discipline, unstable living conditions and other problems within their own environment. But really effective work can pay enormous dividends if young people can be diverted away from adult criminal careers.

CASE STUDY

No case can be claimed to be wholly typical, but Jason Charles (15) who came to the notice of a local young offender team recently, will serve as a useful final example.

Jason was the fifth of six children and lived with his mother, brother and sisters on a large, run-down estate. Conditions at home were difficult—his father had left soon after the birth of the youngest child and, though he had returned some three years later still seemed detached from the rest of the family. He was only rarely in work and poverty was never far away. The two eldest children had left home as soon as they began work and Jason seemed to spend as little time as possible there.

Instead, he drifted into trouble with older youths who were unemployed. They got up late, met in the town centre and stole from shops while one or two of the group created a diversion; in the evenings they were more likely to steal cars and drive them until the petrol tank was empty. It was car offences which had led to Jason's court appearance and, following two cautions, the court had asked for a full pre-sentence report before passing sentence. They were particularly troubled because Jason had been excluded from school (or had simply opted out—it was difficult to tell, although the school were quite relieved that he was no longer attending).

At first, Jason was bored, aimless, hostile and indifferent in turn. He had no vision of the future, no plan for keeping out of trouble and no resources at home which might have helped. Except . . . he *did* have an older sister who had left home and now worked for a local computer firm. Jason thought computer games were 'brilliant'—the only moment of enthusiasm in two long interviews.

Most of what followed can be gauged from the first two supervision plans, made following the court's decision to impose a two year supervision order. They were carefully negotiated and agreed between Jason and the probation officer attached to the Young Offender Team, who had agreed to supervise him. Each had signed it; each had particular responsibilities.

Initial Supervision Plan: February 1998

AIMS   to meet the requirements of the court order
to stop offending
to learn about computers and how to use them properly
to get back to full time school attendance

ACTION

(1) JASON is to report to the Youth Offender Team twice each week for the first month — once, on Tuesdays for individual sessions; once on Thursdays for the Activity Group. After one month, Tuesday reporting remains, he can choose whether to attend on Thursdays.

(2) Jason not to contact the Ferry Road gang (with whom he had got into trouble)

(3) Jason to visit Rita (his sister) every Saturday for a session using her home computer

(4) MR GROVE (the probation officer) to negotiate re-admission to school by the end of the Easter Holidays

(5) to see whether a second-hand computer could be obtained for Jason's own use, subject to one month's attendance at school.

It was the usual mixture of carrot and stick. Jason had admitted over 20 offences and been warned by the court that any further appearance was likely to mean custody. He had already been shaken when two of his co-defendants had each been sent to a young offender institution by the adult court. After a home visit, Mr Grove had decided that little, if any, practical support was likely to be available at home; instead he had spoken to Rita, who had seemed ready to offer help and support. The whole family visited her fairly regularly, but these were to be special Saturday sessions for Jason, to pick up on the legal interest he had shown.

Jason's reporting was fine for a month, and he enjoyed the Activity Group, which allowed for weight lifting, table tennis and other activities. He decided to carry on attending, but individual sessions with Mr Grove, scheduled for Tuesday mornings, were missed. It soon became apparent that old links had not been broken and drugs were often available from the Ferry Road gang. Jason simply couldn't get up the morning afterwards. At the same time, however, tentative negotiations with education colleagues had resulted in a short term agreement for two afternoons attendance at school, one of which would, again, allow access to the computer room.

PROGRESS REPORT AND SUPERVISION PLAN: MAY 1998

Progress Jason is now attending school three days a week and the Behaviour Support Unit of the Education Authority has a special programme, including three hours per week of home tuition, to the end of the summer term. The aim is for full time attendance from September.

Jason no longer sees Rita every Saturday. Instead, her employers have loaned a second-hand computer to him, on which he can work at home (Jason was initially very reluctant as he shared a bedroom and feared the machine might be damaged or stolen). A family meeting with Mr Grove, to which Rita also came, had been needed. Progress in keyboard skills etc. had been excellent.

Reporting arrangements (weekly reporting plus the activity group) to remain until September.

ACTION FOR NEXT THREE MONTHS

JASON (1) to maintain school attendance
(2) to keep to the conditions of the order

MR GROVE (1) to explore whether Summer Holiday computer courses are available
(2) to go, with Jason, to a local archaeological "dig" to see whether Jason would be accepted as a volunteer helper
(3) to have regular family meetings to share progress with Jason's parents

The last of these was a slightly euphemistic way of acknowledging that Jason's home computer—jealously guarded whenever he was there—remained a source of tension. But in the weeks ahead, full time school attendance *was* negotiated and there seemed every chance that Jason's final year could consolidate his progress. The local archaeology society were welcoming at first, but Jason clearly felt uncomfortable and isolated when Mr Grove no longer attended. Jason left a few weeks later, but two members were sufficiently interested in him to maintain contact and Mr Grove welcomed this extra adult help. He feared the long summer break might halt progress and, although a computer course had been found it was for four days only. Then one of Jason's new contacts from the archaeology society offered him odd jobs for pocket money—and suddenly the dull, sullen 15 year old of six months ago was, if not transformed, certainly growing into an interested, articulate young man, ready to talk about his hopes and ambitions.

I asked Adrian Grove for a further progress report before this book was finalised.

If I sound cautious . . . its because all 15 and 16 year olds are so volatile. He's still capable of doing things without thinking; of flying off the handle, of responding to peer pressure. His two co-defendants will be back on the streets soon and I really am worried that he won't steer well clear. I do think he's still at risk of reoffending—but much less than he was. He was really pleased when I said we would soon go to fortnightly reporting; he said it was the first time I'd trusted him!

I think the biggest change is that he's got some legitimate ambitions at last—a proper reason for keeping out of trouble. The school will arrange a work experience placement for him next year—if he behaves himself—and Rita's firm have said they'll take him. He can leave me cold on that computer of his and I guess he's got real talent that he will be able to use.

Well over half the lads on that estate, of his age, have been in trouble and I guess Jason is at risk until he leaves school and gets a job. Growing up there means the odds are stacked against you, but Rita now has a boyfriend who's very good with him—another role model is all to the good.

It's been something of a team effort—he still comes to the Thursday activity group here, not just because it passes the time, but because he gets on well with the couple who run it. The supervision order has really been about building up a framework round him—thank goodness he's had the sense to use it.

ENDNOTE

[1] For a fuller account of youth justice see *Introduction to the Youth Court*, Winston Gordon *et al*, Waterside Press. A new second edition taking account of the changes brought about by the Crime and Disorder Act 1998, the creation of YOTs and the responsibilities of local authorities is available from late 1998/early 1999.

127

CHAPTER 10

Work in the Family Court

The general public rarely associates the probation service with the work of the family courts.[1] Indeed, many people might question the propriety of allowing a service which is closely identified with the criminal justice system to have the responsibility for the Family Court Welfare Service. Yet that is the current position; and 8.5 per cent of the Probation Service's resources is dedicated to this specialist area.

Like so much of the work of the service, it originates in the concept of the probation officer as the independent eyes and ears of the court. In the 1940s, following recommendations from the Denning Committee, a probation officer appointment was made to the High Court to 'investigate and report, at the request of the court, in cases involving disputes over the custody of children'. A 1956 Royal Commission on Marriage and Divorce recommended that this should extend to all divorce cases heard in England and Wales and, as a result, in 1958 probation committees were placed under a statutory duty to appoint divorce court welfare officers.

For many years, most probation officers undertook this work alongside their criminal caseload—not always a happy compromise because of the very difficult negotiations over custody and access agreements which were often involved—but by the 1980s almost all areas had created specialist divorce court welfare teams. They undertook reports for county courts, the 'domestic court' (as it was then known) at magistrates' court level and, when required, for the High Court. They also supervised children made the subject of orders by these courts. The Children Act 1989 transformed the situation, both in terms of practice and language. 'Custody' and 'access' became 'residence' and 'contact' and, if these orders were contested, the task of the family court welfare officer was defined as

> to help the courts in their task of serving the needs of children whose parents are involved in separation or divorce, or whose families are involved in disputes in private law.

A new, short term 'family assistance order' was also introduced for those cases where some additional oversight was needed. Overall, the emphasis moved to stressing the notion of parental responsibility, the needs, wishes and long term interests of the children involved and a conciliatory, rather than an adversarial approach.

128

There had been much criticism of the cumbersome, long drawn out and often bitter disputes which characterised work in this difficult arena; courts were now expected to observe the maxim that delay in matters affecting a child's upbringing was likely to be prejudicial to his or her welfare and that formal court orders would not be made unless absolutely necessary. Despite this, the workload of the courts, and of the Family Court Welfare Service has risen sharply. The recent statistics for family matters (private law applications) dealt with by the courts are as follows:

	1992	1993	1994	1995
Residence	22,601	30,195	32,955	33,954
Contact	26,457	41.742	46,728	51,377

THE MAIN TASKS

These are centred on either the court process, or action required once court decisions have been made.

Court centred
These include:

Directions hearings
Probation officers, known in this setting as family court welfare officers (FCWO) are required, at the request of the court, to meet the parties to make a preliminary assessment of the case and to identify any areas of agreement.

Such meetings are held in advance of the actual court hearing and both the parties and their legal advisers will attend. They are exploratory proceedings so that the FCWO can report to the court on what issues, if any, are in dispute; and whether there is any prospect of agreement being reached, or to what extent, without the continued involvement of the court.

This is pressurised work. Operational and day-to-day arrangements vary considerably between probation areas, but the time allocated to initial directions hearings can vary between 15 minutes and one hour. In some courts, the FCWO sees every case; in others, the judge or justices' clerk pre-selects those cases thought to be appropriate. Where they work well, such proceedings are invaluable—they reduce anxiety and costly court time, restrict equally costly welfare reports to cases where they are really needed and reinforce the notion of parental responsibility.

Mediation

Directions hearings are not *privileged*; that is, the comments of the parties and anyone else present may be reported to the court. Mediation interviews, however, are. The aim is to offer a confidential interview or series of interviews to try and resolve differences, to reinforce parental responsibilities and to try and reach an agreement which is in the best interests of the children.

Such work may be carried out by probation officers, in their role as FCWOs, either at court (and at any stage in legal proceedings) or outside the legal context altogether. Some probation areas work in partnership with national organizations such as Relate, or local Family Mediation services. Both in-court and out-of-court mediation interviews have reduced recently however, in contrast to directions hearings, which are seen to be quicker, cheaper and just as effective. (By the time the parties have got to a contested hearing, experienced FCWOs can assess rapidly whether such meetings are likely to be productive). Recent figures are as follows:

	1992	1993	1994	1995
Mediation (in court)	12,444	16,342	11,116	7,503
Mediation (external)	5,385	6,845	5,635	4,114
Directions hearings	15,208	20,875	29,085	38,902
Welfare reports	23,482	32,805	34,253	34,973

The figure for full welfare reports has been added because one of the main benefits of early intervention, whether by directions hearing or mediation appointments, is to limit the number of written reports, which are both time consuming (around ten weeks is allowed) and expensive (about £880 per report).

WELFARE REPORTS

The preparation of welfare reports is the major task for FCWOs. Such reports are almost always in writing and the court specifies the issues or matters that it wishes to see addressed in the report—although that will not preclude investigation of other matters if the FCWO considers it appropriate. Comprehensive National Standards cover the preparation of such reports, which require the FCWO to 'inquire professionally and impartially into the circumstances of the case in order to discover information likely to assist the court and to report clearly and concisely to the court'. An earlier practice direction was more specific:

Where the court directs an enquiry and report by a welfare officer, it is the function of the welfare officer to assist the court by investigating the circumstances of the child, or children, concerned and the important figures in their lives, to report what (s)he sees and hears, to offer the court an assessment of the situation and where appropriate to make a recommendation. In such circumstances, it is not the role of the welfare officer to attempt conciliation although (s)he may encourage the parties to settle their differences if the likelihood of a settlement arises during the course of enquiries.

Practice Direction [1986] 2 FLR 171

An example of a welfare report is given later in this chapter. Decisions have to be made on whether to see the parties alone or together (the latter requiring the consent of both parties); what home visits should be made and how children should be seen; whether other agencies such as the school, doctor or health visitor should be contacted; and whether other significant individuals, such as a child's carer or the new partner of a parent might contribute.

It is a complex, time consuming and difficult task, often conducted in a highly charged and emotional atmosphere and with both children and parents aware of the impact the eventual court decision will have on their lives. It is perhaps not surprising that, in most probation areas, formal complaints about family court welfare reports are disproportionately high. FCWOs are accused of bias, insensitivity, incompetence and worse simply because, for the disappointed parent, there is little else that he or she can focus anger or blame upon. Scrupulous care has to be taken in investigating these complaints . . . but even then, the outcome may provide little satisfaction.

POST COURT WORK

Family assistance orders
These are made only in exceptional circumstances, with the consent of the adults concerned, and for a maximum of six months. They are designed to help families through a difficult transition period, or to assist in compliance with another order, such as a contact order, where difficulties exist or are likely. The FCWO has authority to return the matter to court for further directions if either party ceases to co-operate. Throughout the order, the welfare of the child, and parental responsibility are guiding principles. Family assistance orders are not always made to the probation service; they may in some circumstances be more appropriately supervised by local

131

authority social services departments. FCWOs in probation areas dealt with 882 such orders in 1995.

Supervision orders

These can be made in care proceedings and are nearly always supervised by the local authority, unless the probation service is, or has been, already involved with another member of the family.

THE CHANGING FACE OF FAMILY LAW

One theme running through this book has been that the only constant is change—and family court work is no exception. The Family Law Act 1996 began a series of changes which may well detach family court work from probation services altogether. The Act recognised the value of mediation and early intervention if divorcing couples were to be helped to resolve their differences outside the court process and made financial provision for it through legal aid.

Information meetings, which parties making the new statement of marriage breakdown must attend, and new mediation arrangements were the focus of most interest, but in neither area were probation areas expected to be involved.

Then, in 1997, the government set up an Inter-Departmental Working Group to look at the future of court welfare services. Options included transfer to a separate and independent agency or to the Lord Chancellors Department, which has direct responsibility for the Courts Service (except for magistrates' courts). Unless the costs of any transfer were excessive, it seemed unlikely that the work would remain with area probation services, although with both primary and secondary legislation needed, a transition period of three to five years would be likely.

For probation services, it would presage enormous change. In 1997/8 the cost of family court work was calculated at £34.7 million, some 8.45 per cent of the cash limit. At present 710 probation officer posts, including managers and senior practitioners, and 272 clerical and administrative posts are involved.

For the moment, however, and for the next few years, the workload is growing and has to be undertaken. How it is done is best explained through examples.

CASE STUDY: COURT WELFARE REPORTS

In the first example, bitter disputes over contact with two small girls had taken both parents back to court. Mrs Graham, who cared for the two girls, (aged seven and four) was hostile to 'staying contact' with her ex-husband (i.e. where the girls could stay overnight with him), claiming that this was disruptive and that the girls were less keen on continuing it as they grew up. She resented the girls' father trying to 'interfere' in schooling matters, too; he was trying to obtain an order from the court which would prohibit a planned change of school. Mr Graham, still devastated by the loss of his children was caring and concerned, but much too emotionally involved to take a more balanced look at the immediate future.

The county court judge, having heard two wholly opposed views, and having seen the absolute commitment of both parents, took the view that the welfare officer should prepare a report in six weeks (all that was left before the start of the autumn term) in terms of schooling, contact, *and* the wishes of the children involved. What followed, as so often happens, was more than simple report preparation. The FCWO used a series of meetings to try and reach some kind of compromise *before* the date of the new hearing. 'No one doubts your love and concern for the girls', he told both parents,

> so why leave it to a judge to make decisions that really should be yours? Now the case has come to court, some kind of decision will have to be made, but it would be much better if it was to approve arrangements that *you* have agreed, and that you know the girls will be happy with. Let's see what we *can* agree on, and go on from there.

The results were reported to the judge as follows.

Persons Interviewed and Sources of Information
In the course of this enquiry I have interviewed Mr Graham at home on two occasions and Mrs Graham twice. I have seen both girls at Mr Graham's home and spoken to them on their own as well as observing contact with their father. I have read all the school reports since Sally started at Valley View Infants School and I have read the School Prospectuses for both Meadows County Junior School and Forest Infants School to which it is proposed that Sally and Rose should, respectively, go from September onwards.

More importantly, during the course of this enquiry, the parents have themselves met and had a long discussion about future arrangements for the children. I have considered these agreed arrangements carefully and discussed them with both Mr and Mrs Graham; I believe them to be in the best interests of the children and they therefore form the basis of this shorter report.

Background

The court will be aware of recent substantial disagreements over contact with the children but it is worth recording that there have, equally, been periods when cooperation has been good and arrangements have been both flexible and effective. Difficulties seem to have surfaced in the autumn of 1996 and got steadily worse until the time of the last court hearing. Both parents link this—in part—to a new relationship formed by Mrs Graham. Her new partner (who also had problems of contact with the child of *his* earlier marriage) moved in with her and the practical and emotional difficulties which then began to surround issues of contact were never properly resolved. That relationship has now ended, leaving both Mr and Mrs Graham able to focus much more clearly on the needs of the children, and with very positive results.

The other background issue worth noting is that Mr Graham has been unusually closely involved with the upbringing of his children. This is more than just being a concerned father—though he is certainly that. He did, however, have a two year period out of work while the children were small and therefore had time, as well as inclination, to be closely involved in their day to day care. The result is a close bond on both sides, readily observable during periods of contact.

The issue I have had to consider is whether any future relationship, entered into by either Mr *or* Mrs Graham would destroy recent progress and cooperation. I think not. Although, after careful discussion with both parents, I think some of the same feelings might resurface, I think both parents have learned from the problems experienced by the children, have a shared determination to avoid them in future and feel that the proposed arrangements will provide a safe framework to enable them to deal with any problems.

Proposed Contact Arrangements

7. The parents have agreed the following:

Arrangements for alternate weekends:-

Weekend (a)	staying contact Friday evening to Sunday evening during school terms
	or
	staying contact Friday evening to Monday morning during school holidays
Weekend (b)	day contact on *either* Saturday or Sunday as agreed.
	Also, during school holidays longer periods of staying contact by agreement.

At the time of writing this report Mr Graham was unemployed and both parents were agreed that this provided a useful opportunity for mid-week staying contact where this seemed appropriate. He does however have a new job and starts on August 21. In the last two weeks arrangements *have* been altered by agreement and I think this flexible approach is to be welcomed. The parents live within a mile or so of each other (about 15-20 minutes walking distance) and it does make this sort of arrangement very much easier to operate.

Schools

Until the end of last term Sally attended Valley View Infants School. She was due to transfer to the junior section of the same school in September and the original assumption was that Rose would then start at the Infants School which, although separate, is on the same site. Sally's progress at school is clear from the annual reports; she is seen as an intelligent child with a good deal of all-round ability, but hampered by a lack of confidence which means that she needs a good deal of support and encouragement to participate in class. When she does so, she contributes well. How much of this uncertainty is due to the problems at home is difficult to assess, but it has probably been a contributing factor. I found her to be a very bright child, good at expressing herself, quick with numbers and writing and I would assess her as being well able to progress in school, wherever she is, if she feels secure.

Mrs Graham determined on a change of school this September for practical reasons. The Meadows and Forest Schools, to which it is proposed the children should go, are — literally — a few hundred yards way; about three minutes walk for an enthusiastic seven year old. Other local children from within a few doors away go there and cooperative arrangements between parents are therefore very much easier. The previous school is acknowledged to have been a good one but needed travel by car (or a much longer walk) and — since a change of school was inevitable, anyway — Mrs Graham decided that this was the least disruptive way of achieving the desired move.

I have had two problems in assessing what might be in Sally's best interest. The first is that, given the timing of the request for this report and the date of the renewed hearing, I have been unable to pursue the matter with the schools concerned. Although I have made contact with both schools it is clear that no teaching staff are due back until August 30 at the earliest and no further information will be available to the court from that source for the renewed hearing. The second is that — not surprisingly — much had already been done to prepare both girls for their new school. Sally, in particular, has spent a half day at Meadows School to familiarise herself with the new surroundings, had met the new headteacher (of whom she approved) and viewed the facilities (about which she was enthusiastic). Both girls talk easily and cheerfully about the change of school and a good deal of care has gone into preparing them for it. It is likely that any abrupt change back would lead to much

135

more uncertainty and would, particularly, be negative in its effect on Sally.

The problem is readily recognised by Mr Graham who had originally objected to the change on the grounds that the existing school was well tried and familiar and that too much was being sacrificed to convenience. He has now, very sensibly, decided to suspend any final judgement until he has been able to visit the new schools and talk to the staff involved. He can do this in the week before Rose starts (on September 12) but Sally, who starts on September 5 will already have started. He and his ex-wife have agreed to discuss it further then, and I have indicated that I would be pleased to be involved if it were felt to be helpful. In the circumstances it seems likely that an order concerning the choice of school ought not to be made and should not be needed.

CHECKLIST
A) Ascertainable wishes and feelings of the children
12. Sally in particular has made it abundantly clear how much she needs and wants both parents. She expresses herself cheerfully, clearly and without reserve; gets real enjoyment from contact with her father, is positive about the new school and will benefit greatly from increased parental cooperation and the proposed new arrangements. Rose manages to be both quieter and more mischievous at the same time. She is developing very much as her own person but still needs the support and contact with her elder sister, who acts as a useful role model.
B) Capabilities of each parent and any other relevant person in meeting the children's needs

There are no problems with either parent—each has a good understanding of what is needed and a real commitment to the well-being of the children. Each, too, has extended family links in the area from which the children will benefit. The only longer term issue will be the physical conditions for staying contact - the house occupied by Mr Graham has only two bedrooms, one of which is his mother's. At present he has a single bed in the same room as the bunk beds occupied by the two girls and eventually this will need to be changed.

There are no other issues arising from the Checklist which need to be detailed here.

Conclusion
Arrangements for contact are now agreed between the parents and the early evidence is that they can and do work well. The extended, flexible contact envisaged is certainly in the best interests of the two children; it is frequent without being disruptive and takes due account of the demands that school will make. An order in the terms described in paragraph 7 above may well be helpful in terms of providing the framework for future cooperation.

In terms of schooling, agreement between the parents does await contact between Mr Graham and the new schools which, for practical reasons, cannot be established until after the projected hearing date. In view of the preparations made (and even Rose has completed a "pre-school preparation pack" in relation to the new school) there would need to be a very clear balance of advantages before a decision that their interests were best served by staying at Valley View Junior and Infants School. It would bring with it a good deal of uncertainty and difficulty, whereas Sally in particular is happy and positive when talking about her new school. Mr Graham recognises this—and has responded as far as he can until he can achieve personal contact with the schools. It may well be that Sally's schooling can be decided amicably and that, at this stage, no order need be made regarding this aspect of the enquiry.

Andrew Headland
Court Welfare Officer

COMMENTARY

In many cases, the disputes over residence and contact are so entrenched that an agreed response to the court is simply not possible. Positions have been taken, battle lines drawn (and, often, grandparents, friends, family doctors and others deployed) to fight the relative merits of particular arrangements up to and beyond the decision by the court. In these unhappy situations parents are, all too often, fighting their own matrimonial battles—the sense of injury and hurt that comes from a fractured relationship is such that compromise cannot be considered.

In these circumstances, FCWOs can only focus on the central part of their task—the long term interests of the children concerned. It requires some delicate judgements about the relative merit of competing arrangements for the children. It also requires some special skills in relation to some of the interviewing needed. Young children must not be put under pressure or asked direct questions which would leave them feeling guilty or exposed to further conflict; they need to be observed, to be listened to in more subtle and careful ways without the burden of making 'choices' which will not be theirs to make. They may also be subject to pressure from either parent and anxious or fearful of the consequences of their position.

It may seem facile to say that children need *both* parents, even if this poses real difficulties, until they can make more mature choices of their own. Yet this simple truth, obscured by circumstances, distance, adult anger and obstructiveness and—above all—the building of relationships with new partners, has to be the starting

137

point for much of the work that FCWOs do. It is not always deliverable, in which case the best compromise possible becomes the aim.

Older children can be expected to be much more direct. They are no respecters of court orders, which they can render unenforceable if they choose, and wise parents, even if they lose out in the short term, will realise this. So many of the conflicts which reach FCWOs are long standing, bitter and almost unresolvable that it would be easy to be depressed by the task. Two balancing factors will help restore a sense of optimism—the first is the regular stream of cases in which a third party (the FCWO) *can* come in, late in the day, and make a difference. Mediation, dispute resolution or even the dogged, patient compromises developed during report preparation can and do make a real impact. The second is that children are astonishingly resilient. They cope with impossible family conflicts (and certainly may be damaged by them) but they often, instinctively, work out survival strategies of their own.

Many probation officers want to keep their involvement with family court work. They see it as complementary to criminal work, for a disturbed or broken home is still a major predictor of criminal offending or other delinquency. They also believe that skills in either setting, as well as understanding, are transferable and that the service as a whole has not valued this enough.

Others—myself included—see the force of the arguments, but think they are outweighed by the benefits of separating into a specialist agency. Parents are confused by the way a primarily criminal agency still deals with family matters; they are often resentful at the labelling this seems to imply. The special skills of working with small children are *not* part of mainstream probation and the degree of re-training needed when staff move in and out of family court welfare posts is a major hazard. Finally, family court welfare work takes up a disproportionate amount of management time in an already complex service.

These counter-arguments have been very apparent for some years. A government review of the structure of family court work was initiated in 1997 and it was made clear then that the likelihood was that it would not remain with the probation service. Closer links with the Lord Chancellor's Department, which has responsibility for the courts, seemed to be one possibility; a completely independent agency another. The costs of any reorganization, however, were likely to come under particular scrutiny when all public expenditure was being limited and, with legislation required for any change, the prospect of an early decision has been receding. At the time of writing

(July 1998) no decisions were known and a three to four year delay before change could be implemented seemed inevitable.

New probation officers are unlikely to experience the work in their first few years. During that time the future of probation involvement in the family courts should at least be decided.

ENDNOTE

[1] For an overview of the hierarchy of family courts and a further outline of the kind of work involved, see *Introduction to the Family Proceedings Court*, Elaine Laken et al, Waterside Press, 1997.

CHAPTER 11

The Future

On 21 July 1998 home secretary, Jack Straw, unveiled new plans for criminal justice agencies in the light of the government's comprehensive spending review and a series of other initiatives aimed at overall crime reduction. Reporting on his statement the following day, *The Times* noted:

> The multi-million pound initiative is to be concentrated on dealing with the social conditions that breed criminal behaviour, targeting criminals and crime "hot spots" and working with offenders.
>
> Mr Straw told M.P's that the police could not fight crime alone and must be helped by local authorities, the Probation Service and magistrates in devising comprehensive strategies to tackle causes and consequences of crime. Mr Straw also announced greater co-ordination between the various arms of the £11 billion a year criminal justice service which involves the police, the Crown Courts and magistrates' courts, the prison and probation services, lawyers and social services. An additional £127 million would go to the Probation Service'.
>
> *The Times,* 22 July 1998

At the same time, final decisions were near on the Prisons-Probation Review, set up a year earlier, to look at ways in which the better integration of the two services could improve their efficiency and performance. The goals were identified as:

- reducing offending
- improved public protection
- greater public confidence in community punishments imposed on offenders, whether as part of a prison sentence or as a community sentence; and
- increased cost effectiveness of programmes and their management.

For the Probation Service it was very much a modernisation agenda, not an abolitionist one and the review covered options for structural change, ways in which prison and probation work might be better integrated, improved strategic planning and even the names, language and terminology in use.

None of this was taking place in a vacuum and it was clear from the final stages leading to the Crime and Disorder Act 1998 how a more coordinated approach would impact upon probation. The youth justice system would be directed by a new National Youth Justice Board with Lord Warner (previously the home secretary's senior policy adviser) as its first chair. Probation services would have to play a central role in the new Youth Offender Teams and as part of local, multi-agency management arrangements. The same 'duty to cooperate' would be equally evident in new community safety plans where, despite statutory responsibility being shared by police and local authorities, probation services would, rightly, be expected to contribute to planning, information-sharing and, above all, the prevention of re-offending.

This new evidence of 'joined-up thinking' is both welcome and overdue. Partnerships between agencies have been common for many years and joint work at all levels has an impressive track record—but it has depended too much on individual initiatives and cooperation and has always been vulnerable to budget and other pressures. All too often, the pressure on one agency from central government to deliver key objectives has been unhelpful to cooperative work. That will take some time to resolve—the fact that police, probation and the Crown Prosecution Service have very different roles is still a factor, for instance —but there is evidence of a much more coherent approach in which the contribution made by individual agencies can fit more effectively together.

Nor are the partnerships all with criminal justice agencies. Drug 'treatment and testing' orders, currently being piloted, will see probation services linked with health service provision; the commercial sector already has an increasing role in electronic monitoring and rehabilitation courses for drink drivers; the voluntary and charitable sector runs a wide range of services and programmes, both residential and non-residential. The key message for probation staff is that the somewhat detached and occasionally isolated work which often characterised probation practice is no longer possible. This is not simply a case of making the best use of community resources—probation staff have been inventive and successful at that for many years—but of working flexibly and interdependently with other partners in the criminal justice process and adopting a more evidence-based approach, with others, to improve both effectiveness and efficiency.

To see what this might mean in practice it is worth separating out three main strands—structure and policy, practice and research, and new technology. The first is largely driven by central government, the second ought to be the province of individual probation areas and the third is already in evidence.

STRUCTURE AND POLICY

Most independent reviews of the Probation Service in the last two decades, from the Audit Commission to foreign visitors, have had little difficulty in identifying both the strengths and weaknesses of the way in which the service operates.

The *strengths* include an impressive level of practice and innovation, a strong local base, including close and productive links with sentencers and a remarkable absence of disasters—given the difficult and often dangerous nature of those supervised—to which other, similar professions have been prone.

The *weaknesses* include the very fragmented nature of the service which has meant, with 54 separate and autonomous areas, a good deal of inconsistency of both provision and practice; a tendency (compounded by a limited research base) to keep reinventing the wheel and failing to spread best practice; and a failure to improve cost effectiveness since every area, both large and small, tends to replicate the same structures.

Cost is a fairly recent issue. While the service was, in comparative terms, very cheap the costs of reorganization hardly seemed justifiable. As probation has grown (the estimated cost for 1997-8 was £429 million) and the pressure on public expenditure has tightened so the benefits of a more cost effective structure have become apparent, and this was certainly a factor in the Prisons/Probation Review. (Comparative costs are, of course, still hugely different. The Home Office report, *Reducing Offending*, quotes Prison Service expenditure for 1997-8 as £1,257 million and the average annual cost of keeping an inmate in prison as £24,000; £37,000 if capital costs were included).

There had also been interesting comparisons with The Netherlands, where a similarly fragmented service had been restructured into far fewer areas, a national director appointed and budget cuts of almost 20 per cent imposed. Five years later, the newly reorganized service has a much larger workload, budgets have almost doubled and—from latest surveys—there is a high level of political and public confidence in the work it undertakes.

Against this background, the Prisons/Probation Review set to work. Its report, concentrating on process and structures, may seem over bureaucratic and far removed from the 'real' world of crime and drugs; family breakdown and divorce; homelessness and poverty. But it is informed by a belief that the right structure *would* improve performance and would deliver policy objectives more consistently. It identified four main possibilities:

• *the 'zero-plus' option* of leaving the current 54 area services in place and thus saving the costs and disruption of reorganization. But it would introduce a much stronger national policy framework than National Standards currently provide; it would look for efficiency gains through improved collaboration and shared services between areas; and a complete package of improvements to improve joint working between prisons and probation. This would include common approaches to information sharing and IT, risk assessment and management, accreditation of offender programmes and joint research and evaluation. Keeping prisoners as near as possible to their home area, linked training and job exchanges and joint performance measurement would be part of the package, too.

• *co-terminosity*, or aligning the Probation Service with police and Crown Prosecution Service boundaries. Common boundaries make a good deal of sense (this would mean 42 areas under present arrangements) and would certainly simplify much operational work as joint agency arrangements become more common. Services would remain separate but could be further grouped in regional structures which would make whole-system planning—in theory—both more efficient and effective.

• *a regional service* based on government regions. This would leave ten regional Probation Services covering vast areas, with staff managed and employed by non-departmental bodies (NDPBs) or 'Next Steps' agencies and a Regional Probation Board headed by its own director. Beneath the regional structure, smaller administrative and operational areas would be needed and might well correspond to the 42 or 54 areas already described. Prison Service areas could also be aligned to a regional model.

• *a national service*, with a national advisory board (as with the new youth justice arrangements) and a chief executive, as the Prison Service has. This would clearly offer more central control and a higher public profile—but economies of scale might well be outweighed by the bureaucracy which would also be necessary. The independent voice which the service currently has would also be lost and it would certainly be more vulnerable to political swings—and, perhaps, extremes.

The consultation period on the prisons-probation review is set to last until the end of November 1998, and views on all the options (but

143

especially the home secretary's preferred option) are likely to be fierce and varied. But change will not necessarily be swift. The need for legislation imposes an automatic brake on the process of change and there is a good deal of scope for debate (and action, at local level) before wholesale change is imminent. Best estimates are that this will not be before 2002 or 2003, depending on the option chosen.

There are gains and losses in all the models. The more centralised the new structure, the more likely that economies of scale can be achieved and consistency of practice improved. But a more remote and bureaucratic hierarchy brings other dangers—less adaptability and responsiveness to local needs; less confidence, perhaps, from local sentencers and communities. The real weakness of the prison-probation review is its assumption that these are the two services which, above all, need the closest links. In reality, a police-probation review, or a local authority-probation review would have been just as appropriate and it is the very close links with a whole *range* of other services and structures which makes anything but a locally based service problematic.

The Woolf Report (1991), which followed the prison disturbances of 1990, had earlier had much to say about the isolation of prisons from other parts of the criminal justice process, not least the Probation Service. It had led to area liaison committees, chaired by judges, but with all *local* agencies involved, in an attempt to improve co-ordination and effectiveness in the system as a whole.

The challenge may be to demonstrate how much improvement can be achieved without large scale re-structuring and the possible loss of very positive local links. A stronger sense of policy direction is already apparent. If that could be enhanced with improved governance and a better framework for local collaboration (and cost sharing) the case for larger scale change might look much less convincing.

A similar situation has arisen with the home secretary's well publicised views on the name 'Probation' and the orders which are supervised. Ministers made it clear that they thought that the term 'probation' had been irreparably damaged and that it was considered too soft and woolly to be retained in an era when a tougher, sharper approach to community penalties was being demanded. The original alternative—a 'Corrections Service' seemed to be abandoned because of unfortunate connotations with Miss Whiplash and other, better known adherents of the term. The prison-probation review came up with eleven alternative horrors including:

• Public Protection Service
• Community Justice Enforcement Service
• Offender Risk Management Service

144

- Public Safety and Offender Management Service; and even
- Justice Enforcement and Public Protection Service.

Yet from the only piece of hard evidence in this 're-branding' exercise, a small survey by MORI commissioned by ACOP, it is clear that the public were comfortable with 'Probation' and that their perception of it and the demands it makes were good. Where the public were confused, and where ministers really do have a point, is in the naming of individual orders. A 'probation order' could equally be a 'community supervision order' and community service orders could become community work orders. These are, at least, accurate descriptions and a change to the latter might reduce the confusion with community service volunteers which currently exists. The combination order is the worst example—a 'community supervision and work order' would, again, describe properly what was involved.

The prisons-probation review accepted that probation is a long-established concept, well understood internationally, and that probation practice in this country enjoys a high reputation. It remains to be seen whether this is sufficient to avoid a change of name, overall, even though changes to individual orders would seem to be the real priority.

Finally, policy matters do need a more consistent and timely approach, whatever structure and names are chosen. One of the more bizarre features of the annual Home Office national plans for the probation service was that, by the time they were published, individual services had already completed the financial processes with their local authorities (since these are fixed by statute) and, with the budget thus set, the chance to respond to the national plan was very limited, if it departed from earlier drafts. A forum in which police, probation, prisons and the health service could meet at national level; decide on joint policy and strategy, agreed targets and standards; could agree resource issues for joint funded work; could work to a consistent planning cycle and commission joint research would be an enormous improvement on the present, fragmented system. Area Criminal Justice Liaison Committees, together with their national body, have been little more than talking shops—useful in liaison terms, but without a strategic edge. If the Probation Service of the future is going to deliver all that is hoped from it, a strong voice in policy matters is going to be an essential starting point. From that point of view, some structural change seems both inevitable and desirable.

PRACTICE AND RESEARCH

As we have seen, the last decade has witnessed a phenomenal increase in the work of the service, including a remorseless rise in throughcare work as prison numbers have increased and this has simply dominated practice. The effect has not been entirely one sided, for the pressure of numbers has made services look to new methods of coping, whether through groupwork, contracting out elements of supervision to other agencies, using volunteers or reintroducing 'reporting schemes' for low risk offenders or those nearing the end of their order. But extra numbers have also kept resources under extreme pressure and curtailed some of the intensive (but expensive) probation schemes which might have been able to contribute more to what we know about reducing re-offending.

In common with all publicly funded services, probation has to demonstrate improved value for money. There are strong demands, too, for more accountability and more consistency to which services have to respond, although these are not limited to probation and apply, equally, across the criminal justice spectrum. The response, which is already well under way has been to concentrate more on core tasks and, especially, to prioritise resource allocation; and to provide an improved framework for service delivery which takes these into account. In general, core tasks might be described as:

- *assessment*, including the preparation of reports for courts, prisons and the Parole Board
- *supervision of orders*
- *public protection and risk management*
- *services to courts.*

These are not, of course, separate and discrete tasks—they all impact on each other. But separating them out enables a closer look at *how* each can be approached. Not all areas will choose the same models but practice developments are likely to be centred on case management, rather than direct casework.

Individual probation officers have always had to rely on a range of specialist services from other colleagues or agencies, whether it concerned psychiatric help, drug and alcohol work, or employment advice. Supervising a case may well mean ensuring that the offender has access to the facilities and expertise he or she needs rather than engaging in a good deal of individual work. But the crucial process of assessment, of agreeing a supervision plan and of monitoring its achievement, as well as compliance with the order needs to be undertaken, reviewed and orchestrated as the order proceeds. It is case management skills which will be needed to ensure that this happens.

Programme provision

The Probation Service is being challenged to demonstrate that supervision uses the most effective programmes and methods—and that they are being applied with commitment and integrity. Such programmes, whether delivered individually or in groups, will become increasingly important; an accreditation process will ensure that they meet demanding criteria in relation to targeting and assessment, programme design and delivery, evaluation and monitoring and even staff training. Will this mean less scope for the skills of individual officers? I think not. However well designed a standard programme is, the *way* in which it is delivered, the quality of interaction and the confidence of staff are still vital ingredients if it is to work well.

Risk assessment

Standardised risk assessment procedures, validated by research, are also likely to be much more widely used. Once again, this might seem to downgrade the skills of the individual officer but in reality it produces a strong and reliable framework against which analysis can be tested. The skill with which information is gained and used will remain vital, for no standard form can cover all the vagaries of human behaviour.

• • •

Whatever the eventual structure for the probation service, it seems to me that a parallel with the development of a national curriculum for schools is appropriate. A strong national framework—and a very prescriptive one, too—but within that overall framework, discretion in terms of local delivery, given the very different conditions and problems which will be encountered in inner cities or rural areas. To work well, central government will need to shed some of its current obsession with detail and with process—clearly defined targets and output measures, with some standardisation of programmes should be the framework within which local services can respond to deliver the national agenda.

The other key component in practice development is research. The Home Office study 'Reducing Re-offending' describes clearly both the paucity of data and its narrowness, pointing out:

Given the increasing emphasis on the ability of community sentences to rehabilitate, it is not surprising that reconviction rates have come to be

147

relied upon as a key measure of their success or failure in reducing offending behaviour.

But it argued for much more broadly based measures because of changes in offence severity or a reduction in the frequency of offending; a lack of attention to key social factors and problems which may have longer-term effects and inconsistent follow-up periods. At both national and local level, that is likely to change.

The home secretary has already announced that £250 million will be available for *evidence-based* work in key areas—dealing with the social conditions which breed criminal behaviour, targeting prolific offenders and crime 'hotspots', and working with offenders. A rigorous approach to monitoring, evaluation and research will be essential if Probation Services are to be part of these developments. Similarly, at the local level, information on re-offending can be combined with locally collected data on specific social problems to enable programme design to meet the needs of offenders—and for results to be tested. The Kent Reconviction Survey (see Further Reading) provides a wealth of examples based on a five year follow up of over 800 offenders and demonstrates clearly the way in which unemployment, drugs and family factors impact on the success or failure of community sentences. By using social factors as well as offence data, both targeting and programme design can be much improved. They are the building blocks of the integrated strategy now being developed by Home Office researchers. Such an approach, with its emphasis on smaller, immediate gains, an accumulation of evidence through pilot projects and improved programme design and long term investment (e.g. with children and families at risk) could not only have substantial benefits— it is likely to shape the work of the probation service of the future.

NEW TECHNOLOGY

Probation and electronic tagging
New technology has already had its impact on the probation service, as in all walks of life. Computerisation of records and case management systems are an obvious example, but the electronic tag, with its direct effect on sentencing and supervision practice shows every sign of being equally important.[1]

The basic tag, normally worn as a bracelet (rather like a slightly oversized wristwatch) on the arm or the ankle, is a sophisticated tamper-proof transmitter which, with a static unit connected to a telephone line in the offender's home, provides information about whether a curfew, usually up to 12 hours a day, is being kept. In this, its

148

most basic form, it does not require the involvement of the probation service once the order is made—commercial contractors monitor compliance with the curfew, follow up any unauthorised absences and return offenders to court if necessary. But probation officers *are* involved in reports to the courts on suitability and may well also be involved with additional reports if the offender has to be resentenced.

However, the 'stand-alone' curfew order, which was introduced in England and Wales on a pilot basis in 1995 is only one option. Courts are able to use it in conjunction with any other community penalty, including a probation order, or while such an order for another offence is still current. Working with the contractors and making the most of the opportunities which the tag provides has therefore been an important area of learning for the Probation Services involved. The pilot projects started in Manchester, Norfolk and Reading but have subsequently been twice extended to nearby areas so that Cambridgeshire, Suffolk, Middlesex and parts of Yorkshire and Lancashire are now included. A national scheme is likely by early 2000.

Tagging has been a small scale option so far, in sentencing terms. Just over 1,400 orders in total had been made by mid-June 1998—but that was in a period of almost three years. As a comparison, in the second year of the trial project, when just over 300 curfew orders were made in the magistrates' courts covered by the scheme, those same courts made 2,900 probation orders, 2,400 community service orders, 900 combination orders—and passed 2,800 prison sentences.

Further growth is likely, however, for two reasons—growing familiarity and, above all, the national extension of the scheme. In January 1999, home detention curfews will allow prisoners serving between three months and four years to be released up to two months early. All those serving sentences of 12 months or more will also be supervised by probation officers as part of their licence period. Current estimates are that over 30,000 prisoners will be released early each year (albeit for relatively short periods), making it the largest single electronic monitoring scheme in the world.

For probation staff the early impact will be in contributing to risk and suitability assessments for those eligible, as well as in maintaining close links with the monitoring providers while joint supervision is in place. What the post-release scheme will achieve, however, is a national infrastructure and since continued expansion should enable unit costs to be reduced there is no doubt that tagging as a sentence, whether or not it is combined with probation or community service, will expand rapidly, too. Probation officers will need to consider the new option in every pre-sentence report they write and are likely to be crucial to the success of the scheme.

Worldwide, tagging has had a very chequered history. Introduced as an attempt to reduce prison populations, it very often increased them, not least because breaches of the order are so faithfully recorded. An emphasis on targeting and being aware of the limitations of the equipment; and a sense of the positive changes which are possible will need to be at the forefront of every pre-sentence report writer's mind. The experience gained in the pilot probation areas should prove particularly useful. The benefits of good liaison and information sharing were soon apparent; the short term impact of the tag introduced a welcome element of control into some very chaotic and disordered lives; and it frequently had the effect of 'buying time' while other, longer term and constructive programmes could begin to take effect.

Tagging is likely to be over used for a time—the appeal of the 'magic bracelet' to politicians has already seen it introduced in the pilot areas for 10-15 year olds, fine defaulters and petty persistent offenders. These have been ill thought through but it will be actual experience which, I hope, will determine whether they continue to expand. Home secretary, Jack Straw, has already agreed (October 1997) that

> We have to recognise that tagging on its own is not significant. It is tagging linked to personal contact with offenders that is likely to be most effective.

It is the Probation Services of England and Wales which will have to demonstrate the truth of that statement.

Tracking schemes
Other developments, too, are waiting in the wings. Sophisticated tracking schemes, which monitor an offender's movements rather than just his or her presence at home, are already available. They use satellite technology but are, at present, bulky, impractical and very expensive, so that usage in the next three years or so is likely to be limited to a few high-profile offenders or experimental schemes. An alternative 'tracking' scheme, using computer-aided voice recognition and telephone technology (which is much cheaper but has other limitations) is about to be tested by Kent Probation Service.

The technology of control has to be understood and used by the Probation Service of the future. How well this can be achieved will have a significant impact on the use of prison *and* community sentences. If all it does is 'toughen up' the way people are dealt with in the community, then there are many dangers. Its capacity for misuse—for increasing rather than decreasing prison populations—is already apparent. But if it can be shown to be an effective way of keeping people out of prison then in terms of both cost and humanity it deserves serious

150

consideration. The probation service will be central to the eventual outcome.

Technology and practice

Working out how new technology can best help the development of probation extends far beyond electronic monitoring. Computerised case management systems are the most obvious example, both in terms of better, more efficient access to information and in savings on administrative and secretarial costs. At their most basic, they have been used to generate letters to offenders as a means of keeping in touch (the huge caseloads overseen by some probation officers in the USA are dependent on this); more sophisticated usage enables a much wider range of information and risk factors to be accessed, and for monitoring systems to be greatly improved. Other examples of developing technology include the use of video reporting booths (where 'contact' is with an interactive screen instead of a human being), voice-print checks by computer and remote drug and alcohol testing. How much these contribute to the overall aim of preventing reoffending has yet to be tested; how much, too, they represent a range of increasingly intrusive controls which simply bring prison into the community is also a matter of concern and debate. The context in which technology is exploited will be just as crucial as the apparatus itself.

For the moment, the more mundane issue is how to develop and exploit a cost-effective computer infrastructure for the probation service, and then to link it with other criminal justice agencies. There is a bewildering range of acronyms to describe current developments— PHOENIX for police and offender records, QUANTUM for the Prison Service, CRAMS for probation and CCCJS for the Home Office which has the eventual aim of ensuring that all agencies have compatible information technology and can support closer joint working with effective data exchange. Experience so far in the Probation Service has not been particularly encouraging, especially in software terms—but the history of large scale computer developments in public bodies should not have encouraged us to expect more. But the infrastructure should be complete by 2000 and national case management software will follow. Making the most of technology is about supporting the most effective work of the human beings on whom probation ultimately depends.

CONCLUSION

In the overall context of criminal justice, probation is a small part of the picture in either resource or staffing terms. But its influence is considerable and is discernible at every stage of the criminal justice process, from crime prevention to post-release supervision. Some 118,000 people started community sentences in 1997; 70,000 were under pre-release or post-release prison throughcare; 36,000 reports were written for family courts and 227,000 reports for criminal courts. This represents an awesome responsibility in terms of the impact on individual lives, as well as for the community as a whole.

Probation staff operate in a climate of changing criminal justice and social policy, and in a multi-cultural society increasingly aware of its obligations to all its citizens. The distinctive contribution which probation can make, by emphasising both the rights and responsibilities of individuals, is needed as much as it has ever been. Its foothold was achieved by earning the trust and confidence of courts; its continued growth depends not just on retaining this but on developing it to embrace the wider community. This book demonstrates, I hope, just how much of that has already been achieved over the years and, particularly, in recent times. Current debates on criminal justice issues also indicate how much more still needs to be done—and the potential which probation has to achieve still more.

ENDNOTE

[1] For a comprehensive treatment see *Tackling the Tag: The Electronic Monitoring of Offenders,* Waterside Press, 1997.

Appendix I

Qualifying Training for the Probation Service

After a difficult period with no qualifying training procedure in place, new national arrangements for the Diploma In Probation Studies (DipPS) are scheduled to start in the Autumn of 1998. These will be delivered via nine consortia of probation services, organized on a regional basis; their addresses are included below.

The new diploma will be both a higher education degree award and an NVQ Level 4 award in Community Justice. Recruitment and selection will be organized through the regional consortia but individual probation areas will still have a key role, since those successful will become Trainee Probation Officers, and be employed by a specific area service. For this reason, the full list of area probation services is also given, in *Appendix II*.

Small numbers mean that there is unlikely to be a single, set course in each region. Instead, individually designed pathways will enable a much more flexible approach to be adopted, which can accredit prior learning, whether academic or based on practical experience. Individual, taught modules will use small groups at different locations within the consortium area and local support groups for trainees will also be organized.

Practice teaching – 'on the job placements' will account for about half of the time spent on the Diploma in Probation Studies, which is expected to take an average of two years to complete. Practice Development Assessors (PDA's) will supervise the work of trainees, who are likely to be part of the local teams where experience is to be gained. Placements in field teams, prison probation units, hostels, groupwork teams and others will all be used. The following outline gives the core syllabus for the diploma:

Phase I – Modules on:	Orientation to the Criminal Justice System and legal institutions. Foundation skills and methods Values and ethics The learning process and professional development Introduction to the Social Sciences (crime and criminology, the social context, social science methodology) Plus Foundation practice (50 per cent of *Phase I*)
Phase II – Modules on:	The legal and policy framework Understanding crime and criminology

153

Understanding social problems
Developing effective practice
Addressing crime and its effects
Supervising, managing and enforcing community programmes
Assessing offending behaviour and risk
Addressing offending behaviour and managing risk
Working in an organizational context
Professional development
Plus, again, *practice experience* for approximately 50 per cent of *Phase II*.

The educational qualifications for entry to the scheme will *generally* be:

- **Candidates under 21** Minimum of two A-level passes and three at GCSE *or* three at A-level and one at GCSE
- **Candidates 21-25** Generally, five passes at GCSE
- **Candidates over 25** Acceptance without formal qualifications is possible subject to written assessment.
(These need to be checked with individual consortia as some slight variations may occur).

To summarise, DipPS trainees will have to follow a dedicated path of study and undertake the mandatory NVQ units that are required to become a probation officer. The NVQ will receive academic credits which will make up a percentage of the credits to achieve a degree. The remainder of the credits for the degree will be gained by completing the academic modules noted above.

Trainees will be employed by individual area probation services and will have no other responsibilities during their period of training. The minimum starting salary (as at June 1998) will be at point 70 of the national 'single salary spine' (i.e. £11,436) with flexibility to enhance this by six percentage points to reflect previous experience, in appropriate cases. An additional three percentage points are available after one year as a trainee.

Hours of work per week will be 37; with leave at 20 days per year. (Existing probation service staff who transfer to the new scheme will retain 'continuous service'conditions and could thus qualify for 25 days leave if they had five years existing service). All training expenses are met by the employer.

Trainees are asked for a preference in terms of the area in which they would like to work. Since some will be mobile, or able to consider a number of different geographical areas, the standardised application procedure will greatly simplify multiple applications.

Addresses
The Training Managers and consortium addresses, for further information, are as listed opposite:

London Consortium
(covering Inner London, Middlesex and NE, SW and SE London Probation Services), c/o Inner London Probation Service, Mitre House, 223-237 Borough High Street, London SE1 1JD.   Tel: 0171 233 2024

North of Thames
(Cambridgeshire, Essex, Hertfordshire, Norfolk, Northamptonshire, Suffolk, Bedfordshire), c/o Hertfordshire Probation Service, Leahoe House, County Hall, Hertford SG13 8EH.   Tel: 01992 504444

South East
(Berkshire, Hampshire, Kent, Oxford and Buckinghamshire, Surrey, East Sussex, West Sussex), c/o Guildford Probation Centre, College House, Woodbridge Road, Guildford GU1 4RS.   Tel: 01483 860191

South West
(Avon, Cornwall, Devon, Gloucestershire, Somerset, Wiltshire, Dorset), c/o Dorset Probation Service, Court Buildings, Worgret Road, Wareham BH20 6BE.   Tel: 01929 553333

Wales
(Dyfed, Mid, South and West Glamorgan, Gwent, Powys and North Wales), c/o Mid Glamorgan Probation Service, Brackla House, Brackla Street, Bridgend CF31 1BZ.   Tel: 01656 766336

Midlands
(Derbyshire, Hereford and Worcester, Leicestershire, Lincolnshire, Nottinghamshire, Shropshire, Staffordshire, Warwickshire, West Midlands), c/o West Midlands Probation Service, 1 Victoria Square, Birmingham B1 1BD.   Tel: 0121 631 3484

North East
(Durham, Northumbria, Teeside), c/o Teeside Probation Service, 2nd Floor, Prudential House, 31-33 Albert Road, Middlesborough TS1 1PE. Tel: 01642 230533

North West
(Cheshire, Cumbria, Lancashire, Greater Manchester, Merseyside), c/o Merseyside Probation Service, 1c Derby Lane, Old Swan, Liverpool L13 6QA.   Tel: 0151 280 0161

Yorkshire and Humberside
(Humberside; North, West and South Yorkshire), c/o Humberside Probation Service, 1 Airmyn Road, Goole, North Humberside, DN14 6XA. Tel: 01405 767177

Appendix II
Useful Addresses

Probation Areas in England and Wales, Northern Ireland, Jersey, Guernsey, Isle of Man

Area	CPO	
Avon Brunel House, 83 Newfoundland Road Bristol BS2 9LU	**Kay Foad**	Tel: 0117 983 0000 *Fax: 0117 983 0052*
Bedfordshire 3 St Peter's Street, Bedford MK40 2PN	**John Scott**	Tel: 0123 421 3541 *Fax: 0123 432 7497*
Berkshire 145 Friar Street, Reading RG1 1EX	**Andrew Bridges**	Tel: 0173 457 4091 *Fax: 0173 458 8394*
Cambridgeshire Godwin House, Castle Street Cambridge CB3 0RA	**John Hughes**	Tel: 0122 335 9443 *Fax: 0122 331 5657*
Cheshire 17 Cuppin Street, Chester CH1 2NB	**Andrew Taylor**	Tel: 0124 431 2333 *Fax: 0124 431 7318*
Cornwall 22 Lemon Street, Truro TR1 2LS	**Colin Bridges**	Tel: 01872 260 032 *Fax: 01872 272 349*
Cumbria Lime House, The Green Wetheral Carlisle CA1 8EW	**Ian White**	Tel: 0122 856 0057 *Fax: 0122 856 1164*
Derbyshire 18 Brunswood Road, Matlock Bath Matlock DE4 3PA	**Steve Goode**	Tel: 0162 955 422 *Fax: 0162 958 0838*
Devon Queen's House, Little Queen Street Exeter EX4 3LJ	**Diane Shepherd**	Tel: 01392 474 100 *Fax: 01392 413 563*
Dorset Wadham House, 50 High Street West Dorchester DT1 1UT	**Barrie Crook**	Tel: 0130 525 1000 *Fax: 0130 522 5097*

Durham   **Pam McPhee**   Tel: 0191 384 9083
Forest House, Aykley Heads Business Park   *Fax: 0191 374 6958*
Durham DH1 5TS
Dyfed   **Geoffrey Cartledge**   Tel: 0126 722 1567
Llangunnor Road, Carmarthen SA31 2PD   *Fax: 0126 722 1566*

East Sussex   **Penny Buller**   Tel: 0127 369 5327/8
6 Pavilion Parade Brighton BN2 1RA   *Fax: 0127 362 0581*

Essex   **Martin Wargent**   Tel: 0137 650 1626
Cullen Mill, 49 Braintree Road   *Fax: 0137 650 1174*
Witham CM8 2DD

Gloucestershire   **Gill Mackenzie**   Tel: 0145 242 6250
Bewick House, 103 London Road   *Fax: 0145 242 6239*
Gloucester GL1 3HN

Greater Manchester   **Christine Knott**   Tel: 0161 872 4802
Oakland House, Talbot Road   *Fax: 0161 872 3483*
Manchester M16 0PQ

Guernsey   **Barbara Workman**   Tel: 10481 724337
St James Street, St Peter Port   *Fax: 01481 710545*
Guernsey GY1 2NZ

Gwent   **Peter Sampson**   Tel: 0149 576 2462
Cwmbran House Mamhilad Park Estate   *Fax: 0149 576 2461*
Pontypool NP4 0XD

Hampshire   **Stephen Murphy**   Tel: 0196 284 2202
Friary House, Middle Brook Street   *Fax: 0196 286 5278*
Winchester SO23 8DQ

Hereford & Worcs   **Jenny Roberts**   Tel: 0190 572 3766
3/4 Shaw Street, Worcester WR1 3QQ   *Fax: 0190 529 057*

Hertfordshire   **Geoffrey Dobson**   Tel: 0199 250 4444
Leahoe House, County Hall   *Fax: 0199 250 4544*
Hertford SG13 8EH

Humberside   **Hilary Thompson**   Tel: 0148 286 7271
21 Flemingate, Beverley   *Fax: 0148 286 4928*
North Humberside HU17 0NP

Isle of Man   **David Sellick**   Tel: 0162 468 6579
Government Buildings Lord Street   *Fax: 0162 468 6569*
Douglas, Isle of Man M1 1LE

Inner London	**John Harding**	Tel: 0171 222 5656
71/73 Great Peter Street, London SW1P 2BN		*Fax: 0171 233 1305*
Jersey	**Debbie King**	Tel: 0153 433 261
13/15 Don Street, St Helier Jersey JE4 8YZ		*Fax: 0153 458 796*
Kent	**Dick Whitfield**	Tel: 0162 275 0934
58 College Road, Maidstone ME15 6SJ		*Fax: 0162 268 8004*
Lancashire	**John Crawforth**	Tel: 0177 220 1209
99/101 Garstang Road, Preston PR1 1YZ		*Fax: 0177 288 4399*
Leicestershire	**Tony Raban (acting)**	Tel: 0116 251 6008
2 St John Street, Leicester LE1 3BE		*Fax: 0116 251 2801*
Lincolnshire	**Sheridan Minshull**	Tel: 0152 252 3308
7 Lindum Terrace, Lincoln LN2 5RP		*Fax: 0152 252 7685*
Merseyside	**David Mathieson**	Tel: 0151 920 9201
Burlington House, Crosby Road North		*Fax: 0151 949 0528*
Liverpool L22 0PJ		
Middlesex	**John Walters**	Tel: 0171 436 7121
Glen House 200, Tottenham Court Road		*Fax: 0171 436 9827*
London W1P 9LA		
Mid Glamorgan	**Samuel Pollock**	Tel: 0165 676 6336
Brackla House, Brackla Street		*Fax: 0165 276 7296*
Bridgend CF3 1BZ		
Norfolk	**Mary Reed**	Tel: 0160 322 0100
4th Floor St James' Yarn Mill		*Fax: 0160 366 4019*
Whitefriars Norwich NR3 1SU		
N E London	**Howard Lockwood**	Tel: 0181 514 5353
4th Floor, Olympic House *Fax: 0181 478 4450*		
28/42 Clements Road Ilford IG1 1BA		
North Wales	**Carol Moore**	Tel: 0149 251 3413
Alexandra House Abergele Road		*Fax: 0149 251 3373*
Colwyn Bay, Clwyd LL29 9YF		
North Yorkshire	**Roger King**	Tel: 0160 977 8644
Thurstan House, 6 Standard Way		*Fax: 0160 977 8321*
Northallerton DL6 2XQ		

Northamptonshire	**Ellie Roy**	Tel: 0160 435 274
53 Billing Road Northampton NN1 5DB		*Fax: 0160 423 1730*
Northern Ireland	**Briedge Gadd**	Tel: 012 326 2400
80/90 North Street, Belfast BT1 1LD		*Fax: 012 326 2470*
Northumbria	**Michael Worthington**	˙Tel: 0191 281 5721
Litton House, Eslington Road		*Fax: 0191 281 3548*
Jesmond Newcastle upon Tyne NE2 4SP		
Nottinghamshire	**David Hancock**	Tel: 0115 935 1011
Castle Marina Road, Nottingham NG7 1TP		*Fax: 0115 935 1015*
Oxfordshire/	**Eithne Wallis**	Tel: 0186 925 5300
Buckinghamshire		*Fax: 0186 925 5355*
Kings Clere Road, Bicester OX6 8QD		
Powys	**Neil Carter**	Tel: 0159 782 3061
The Limes, Temple Street		*Fax: 0159 782 4657*
Llandrindod Wells LD1 5EA		
Shropshire	**Roger Ford**	Tel: 0174 323 5013
Abbeydale House, 39 Abbey Foregate		*Fax: 0174 323 6172*
Shrewsbury SY2 6BN		
Somerset	**David Clitheroe**	Tel: 0182 325 9474
6 Mendip House, High Street		*Fax: 0182 333 2740*
Taunton TA1 3SX		
S E London	**David Hill**	Tel: 0181 464 3430
Crosby House, 9/13 Elmfield Road		*Fax: 0181 466 1571*
Bromley BR1 1LT		
South Glamorgan	**Peter Trusler**	Tel: 0122 223 2999
Suite 2, St David's House, Wood Street		*Fax: 0122 223 0384*
Cardiff CF1 1EY		
S W London	**David Chantler**	Tel: 0181 546 0018
45 High Street		*Fax: 0181 549 8990*
Kingston upon Thames KT1 1LQ		
South Yorkshire	**John Hicks**	Tel: 0114 276 6911
11a Arundel Gate, Sheffield S1 2PQ		*Fax: 0114 275 2868*
Staffordshire	**David Walton**	Tel: 0178 522 3416
28 Salter Street, Stafford ST16 2LS		*Fax: 0178 522 3108*

Suffolk **Arnold Barrow**		Tel: 0147321 0675
Foundation House, 34 Foundation Street		*Fax: 0147 323 6216*
Ipswich IP4 1ST		

Suffolk   **Arnold Barrow**   Tel: 0147321 0675
Foundation House, 34 Foundation Street   *Fax: 0147 323 6216*
Ipswich IP4 1ST

Surrey   **Michael Varah**   Tel: 0148 386 0191
Bridge House, The Wharf   *Fax: 0148 386 0295*
Godalming GU7 1JB

Teesside   **Roger Statham**   Tel: 0164 223 0533]
Prudential House, 31/33 Albert Road   *Fax: 0164 222 0083*
Middlesborough TS1 1PE

Warwickshire   **Philip Robson**   Tel: 0192 641 1222
2 Swan Street, Warwick CV34 4BJ   *Fax: 0192 640 3183*

West Midlands   **Eric Morrell**   Tel: 0121 631 3484
1 Victoria Square, Birmingham B1 1BD   *Fax: 0121 631 3749*

West Sussex   **David Scott**   Tel: 0124 378 8299
61 North Street, Chichester, PO19 1NB   *Fax: 0124 353 2076*

West Yorkshire   **Anne Mace**   Tel: 0192 436 4141
Cliff Hill House, Sandy Walk   *Fax: 0192 438 2256*
Wakefield WF1 2DJ

Wiltshire   **Chris Wheeler**   Tel: 0122 571 3666
Rothermere, Bythesea Road   *Fax: 0122 571 3995*
Trowbridge BA14 8JQ

West Glamorgan   **Jeff Collins**   Tel: 0163 963 9934
Pearl Assurance House, 119 London Road   *Fax: 0163 964 1675*
Neath SA11 1LG.

National Organizations

ASSOCIATION OF CHIEF OFFICERS OF PROBATION (ACOP)
212 Whitechapel Road, LONDON E1 1BJ   Tel: 0171 377 9141
ACOP is open to all chief officer grade staff and to senior administrative personnel. A national council is elected, which is responsible for the general conduct of the Association's affairs, including decisions on policy, priorities and relations with the media and other organisations. 'Lead officers' are appointed on a wide range of subject areas and position statements are issued on a variety of important topics, eg the supervision of sex offenders, domestic violence or electronic monitoring. ACOP publishes a range of literature and also organises seminars and training events.

CENTRAL PROBATION COUNCIL (CPC)
38 Belgrave Square, London, SW1X 8NT   Tel: 0171 245 9480/9364
CPC represents Probation Committees throughout England and Wales, and the Probation Board for Northern Ireland. It thus represents the employers of probation staff. It works closely with ACOP and has main objectives covering recruitment, training, pay and conditions of service; representing committees to central government and others; and promoting understanding of the work of the service.

HOME OFFICE (PROBATION UNIT)
50 Queen Anne's Gate, LONDON SW1H 9AT   Tel: 0171 273 4000
The Probation Unit is part of the Criminal Policy Directorate of the Home Office. A Home Office minister (currently Lord Williams of Mostyn) has particular responsibility for prison and probation matters. Within the unit there are separate sections dealing with

- Resources (including human resources and training)
- Policy (criminal law, supervision, reports and partnerships)
- Projects (including computerisation and electronic monitoring).

NATIONAL ASSOCATION OF PROBATION OFFICERS (NAPO)
3/4 Chivalry Road, Battersea, LONDON SW11 1HT   Tel: 0171 223 4887
NAPO is a TUC affiliated trade union and represents a wide range of probation service staff. It negotiates pay and conditions of service for probation officer and senior probation officer staff and (jointly with UNISON) for other service grades, except chief officers. It is also a professional and campaigning organisation, working towards improving the work of the probation service and influencing legislation in the criminal justice and social policy fields.

Other Organizations and Interest Groups

ASSOCIATION OF BLACK PROBATION OFFICERS
289 Borough High Street, LONDON SE1 1JG

NATIONAL ASSOCIATION OF ASIAN PROBATION STAFF
53 Billing Road, Northampton NN1 5DB

APEX CHARITABLE TRUST LTD
St Alphage House, Wingate Annexe, 2 Fore Street, LONDON EC27 5DA
Advice and guidance, especially on employment to ex-offenders.

CENTRAL COUNCIL FOR EDUCATION & TRAINING IN SOCIAL WORK
Derbyshire House, St Chads Street, LONDON WC1H 8AD

PROBATION MANAGERS ASSOCIATION
Hayes Court, West Common Road, Bromley, Kent BR2 7AU

SOCIETY OF VOLUNTARY ASSOCIATES
350 Kennington Road, LONDON SE11 4LH
Recruits and trains members of the community to work with offenders and their families.

VICTIM SUPPORT
Cranmer House, 39 Brixton Road, LONDON SW9 6DZ
Co-ordinates the work of local groups providing services to victims of crime and their families.

Appendix III

National Standards: A Summary

This appendix is based on the current National Standards booklet, issued in 1995. It is the single most important framework document for probation staff, since it sets out explicitly the expectations of central government in terms of how supervision and other tasks should be undertaken. National Standards are not set in tablets of stone—these are the second full version, following an earlier trial with community service—and they will no doubt be amended again before too long. There may also be minor variations in the way the standards are used at local level—a product not just of local conditions, but also reflecting the fact that many probation areas had local 'standards' documents and policies well before the national ones appeared.

National Standards cover the *quantity* and *scope* of contact comprehensively. What they cannot do is tell you about *quality*, that all-important and hard-to-define 'extra' which makes the difference, say, between an indifferent and a purposeful interview. So this summary comes with several health warnings:

- never mistake quantity for quality—but, equally, never underestimate the value of quantity, either. Frequent reporting, even if it ends up seeming boring or even punitive, is a repeated reminder of the bargain with the court which must be kept
- never be afraid to make sound professional judgements. National Standards are a framework, not a straitjacket and if staff wish to use their discretion, there is no reason why they should not do so. The *reasons* for doing so should be recorded, of course, and approval may need to be sought. Proper accountability is a safeguard for both officer and offender
- National Standards don't provide answers—but they do help in asking the right questions

The full title of the standards is 'National Standards for the Supervision of Offenders in the Community' (1995) (obtainable from the Home Office: see *Appendix II: Useful Addresses*). A separate booklet covers Family Court Welfare Work. Apart from some general issues (including record keeping, inspection and monitoring, equal opportunities) it covers:

- Pre Sentence Reports
- Probation Orders
- Supervision Orders
- Community Service Orders
- Combination Orders
- Supervision before and after release from custody
- The management of approved probation and bail hostels
- Bail Information schemes.

163

Since these are all covered in more detail in the relevant chapters in this book an explanation of the requirements is not necessary here. But there are key requirements, particularly in terms of frequency and speed of contact, which are regularly monitored by both the Home Office and local probation areas, and annual 'performance indicator' targets for meeting them are also set. The following diagram lists the main targets.

Order	First Contact Within	Home Visit Required?	Minimum Contacts First 3 Months	Minimum Contacts 3-6 Months	Report or Supervision Plan Completed by
Pre Sentence Report	2 days	Yes	2	n/a	15 days
Probation	5 days	Yes	12	6	10 days
Supervision Order	5 days	Yes	12	6	10 days
Community Service Order	10 days	No	Min. 5 - Max. 21 hours per week		n/a
Prison Licence	24 hours	in 5 days	Second contact by 10 days weekly contact (min) for 4 weeks; fortnightly (min) for months 2 and 3		10 days

National Standards also provide useful *check lists*, which cover everything from paragraph headings in pre-sentence reports to the items which must be covered in the first meeting in a new probation order; methods of working and the *content of the supervision plan*, where the requirements are:

• to identify the offender's motivation, pattern of offending, relevant problems/needs, the risk of reoffending or serious harm to the public, and the requirements of the order
• to identify work to be done to make offenders aware of the impact of their offences on their victims, themselves and the community
• to describe the purpose and desired outcomes of supervision
• to set out the individual programme to be followed, including specific objectives, methods and timescale; and
• to specify how, and how often, contact is to be maintained.

It is, like the rest of National Standards, a comprehensive approach. Its weakness is its failure to recognise the chaotic, disordered lives led by so many offenders — and the demands that this makes on the conduct of the order. Offenders rarely follow the orderly pattern envisaged by National Standards . . . But they act as a template, improve consistency and have helped sentencers to retain their confidence in community sentences. The claim in the introduction to the National Standards booklet is that they provide 'a framework for good practice and a basis for demonstrating accountability and achievement'. These have certainly been needed as the *Citizens Charter* and other initiatives have established clear standards for public services. Within that framework, probation staff can still exercise the initiative and professional judgement that really makes a difference.

Appendix IV

Further Reading

This is not intended as a comprehensive bibliography, or a specialised reading list. I have deliberately restricted it to key texts for the general reader or for the prospective applicant who wants to know more. Because of the pace of change I have also not considered publications prior to the Criminal Justice Act of 1991 — however good they are, and some are very good indeed) they describe a different landscape.

Community Service Orders: An Undervalued Sentence (pamphlet), Howard League: London, 1997

Crime, Criminal Justice and the Probation Service, Robert Harris, Routledge: London, 1992

Criminal Justice in Transition, Bryan Gibson *et al*, Waterside Press: Winchester, 1994

Effective Probation Practice , Raynor P, Smith D, and Vanstone, M, Macmillan: London, 1994

Introduction to the Criminal Justice Process, Paul Caradino and Bryan Gibson, Waterside Press: Winchester, 1995

National Standards for the Supervision of Offenders in the Community, Home Office: London, 1995

Offenders on Probation, Home Office Research Study No. 167, G Mair and C May, Home Office: London, 1997

Paying Back: Twenty Years of Community Service, Dick Whitfield and David Scott (Eds.), Waterside Press: Winchester, 1993

Probation: Working for Justice, Ward, D and Lacey, M (Eds.), Whiting and Birch: London, 1995

Reducing Offending, Home Office Research Study No. 187, C Nuttall (Ed.), Home Office: London, 1998

Strategies for Effective Offender Supervision, Andrew Underdown, Home Office: London, 1998

The Kent Reconviction Survey: A Five Year Follow-up Study, Mark Oldfield, Kent Probation Service: Maidstone, 1996

The Probation Handbook, Jones A., Kroll B, Pitts J, Smith P and Weise B, Longmans: London, 1992

The Sentence of the Court, Michael Watkins *et al*, Waterside Press, Winchester, 1998

The Work of Prison Probation Departments: A Thematic Inspection, Probation Inspectorate Report, Home Office: London, 1996.

Readers are also referred to the texts mentioned at the end of certain chapters which contain further, specialist information.

Appendix V The Sentencing Framework

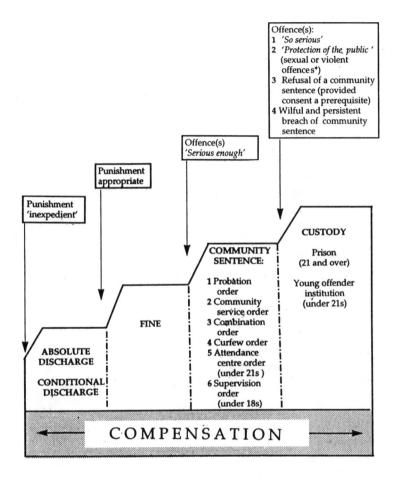

Reproduced courtesy of the authors of *The Sentence of the Court,* Waterside Press, 1998

Further explanation is contained at pages 49 to 50 of this handbook

*References to sexual or violent offences are to such offences as defined in the Criminal Justice Act 1991 (as amended).

Index

The Magistrates Bench Handbook

An invaluable resource for anyone interested in magistrates' courts. Developed in partnership with:

- The Judicial Studies Board
- The Magistrates' Association
- The Justices' Clerks' Society.

The handbook comprises a binder, 232 loose-leaf A4 pages concerning adult offenders in the magistrates' court and section dividers. It includes:

1. **Introduction** With a Foreword by **Lord Irvine of Lairg, Lord Chancellor**
2. **The Sentence of the Court** The main text of the second edition. Foreword by **Lord Bingham, Lord Chief Justice***
3. **Guidelines:**
- *The Magistrates' Association Sentencing Guidelines*
- *National Mode of Trial Guidelines*
- *Considerations Affecting Decisions Whether or Not to Commit to the Crown Court for Sentence.*

4.Decision-making A range of core materials:
JSB Structured Decision-making Charts:
Case Management
Bail or Custody
Venue for Either Way Offences
Guilty or Not Guilty
Sentencing
Fine Enforcement.

Reference Sheets:
Equality of Treatment
Maximum Penalties Etc
Penalty Points and Disqualification
Order of Proceedings
Contempt of Court
Costs
The Public, The Press and Reporting Restrictions
Search Warrants
Appeals and Re-opening of Decisions
PSD Licensing
Words and Jargon
Possible Future Sentencing Changes
Offenders Below 18 Years of Age
Natural Justice.

(1998) ISBN 1 872 870 62 7 £35 per copy plus £3.50 p&p (UK only)
* Alternatively, *The Sentence of the Court* on its own is available in paperback at £12 plus £1.50 p&p: ISBN 1 872 870 64 3

Principled Policing: Protecting the Public With Integrity John Alderson

As John Alderson demonstrates, it is all too easy for quite 'ordinary' police officers to descend into behaviour which is difficult to comprehend – as a result of working cultures, state manoeuvring and the lack of fundamental values for police work. Through his description of what he calls 'high police' and by way of worldwide examples – from Northern Ireland to Tiananmen Square, Nazi Germany to J. Edgar Hoover's days at the FBI and the British miners strike of 1984/5 – the author calls for decency, fairness and morality to act as touchstones for police officers everywhere.

A central appeal of *Principiled Policing* lies with its straightforward message that "good policing" flows from sound principles. The principles that John Alderson recommends to us are bound to notions of justice, fairness, tolerance and a deep sense of community. He has been preaching these principles for many years. We have not always had the sense to listen. As we enter an era in which criminal justice policy is re-built around a concern for 'social exclusion' and a heavy commitment to social crime prevention and 'partnership', we should go back to the writings of John Alderson. He was right all along. From the *Foreword* by **Professor Stephen Savage**, University of Portsmouth

John Alderson CBE, QPM, barrister-at-law is a police writer and scholar whose work is of international repute. His books and papers have been translated into many languages (from Icelandic to Chinese) and are in use in police institutions worldwide. He was formerly Chief Constable of Devon and Cornwall.

(1998) ISBN 1 872 870 71 6. £18 plus £1.50 p&p

Drugs, Trafficking and Criminal Policy: The Scapegoat Strategy Penny Green

A survey of drugs policy which explores the actual nature of events by focusing on drug trafficking and drug traffickers. Penny Green demonstrates that the vast majority of people arrested, convicted and imprisoned for drug trafficking offences are low-level players – causing her to argue that scapegoating has played a central role in shaping the criminal justice drugs war. It is those people at the bottom end of the drugs trade who give substance to its ideology and reality. The author argues that unless drug control moves beyond its present emphasis – and beyond criminal policy and law enforcement into the arena of geo-political analysis, international poverty, Third World debt and domestic welfare – there can be no resolution to the human tragedy which the war on drugs has come to embody.

Penny Green is Director of the Institute of Criminal Justice at the University of Southampton and a Senior Lecturer in Law.

(1998) ISBN 1 872 870 33 3. £18 plus £1.50 p&p

The Waterside Press Introductory Series

☐ **Introduction to the Criminal Justice Process** Bryan Gibson and Paul Cavadino. A complete overview of criminal justice. Rarely, if ever, has this complex process been described with such comprehensiveness and clarity *Justice of the Peace* (Reprinted 1997) ISBN 1 872 870 09 0. £12

☐ **Introduction to the Magistrates' Court** Bryan Gibson With a *Glossary of Words, Phrases and Abbreviations*. An ideal introduction *Law Society Gazette*. (1995) ISBN 1 872 870 15 5. £12. **A new enhanced third edition including** *Basic Procedures and Evidence* **is scheduled for early 1999.**

☐ **Introduction to the Youth Court** Winston Gordon, Michael Watkins and Philip Cuddy. **Foreword: Lord Woolf, Master of the Rolls** A must for those interested in the work of the youth courts *The Magistrate*. Extremely useful and practical *The Law*. (1996) ISBN 1 872 870 36 8. £12. **A new enhanced second edition is scheduled for early 1999.**

☐ **Introduction to the Probation Service** Dick Whitfield. A fully updated second edition of Anthony Osler's original work, including the Prisons/Probation Review and the effects of the Crime and Disorder Act 1998. (1998) ISBN 1 872 870 73 2 £12

☐ **Introduction to Prisons and Imprisonment** Nick Flynn **Foreword: Lord Hurd.** Under the auspices of the Prison Reform Trust. ISBN 1 872 870 37 6. £12

☐ **Introduction to Criminology** Russell Pond A basic guide for lay people written with those working in the criminal justice arena in mind. The main strands of criminology and their sources. ISBN 1 872 870 42 2. £12

☐ **Introduction to the Scottish Childrens Panel** Alistair Kelly Very interesting reading *The Law*. ISBN 1 872 870 38 4. £12.

☐ **Introduction to Road Traffic Offences** Winston Gordon, Philip Cuddy (1998) ISBN 1 872 870 51 1. £12

☐ **Introduction to the Family Proceedings Court** Elaine Laken, Chris Bazell and Winston Gordon. **Foreword: Sir Stephen Brown**. Because of its clarity of information and its lucidity of language and explanation *Introduction to the Family Proceedings Court* is a very accessible handbook *The Magistrate*. (1997) ISBN 1 872 870 46 5. £12

☐ **Conflict Resolution: A Basic Guide** Susan Stewart A wide ranging look at constructive ways of resolving disputes. ISBN 1 872 870 65 1 £12

An invaluable resource